PRINT MAKING *without a Press*

PRINT MAKING *without a Press*

Janet Doub Erickson   *Adelaide Sproul*

Reinhold Publishing Corporation / New York
an Art Horizons book

54520

Tree by Carol Summers. Color plywood print. (See page 80.)

© 1966, Art Horizons, Inc.
All rights reserved
Printed in the United States of America
Library of Congress Catalog Card No. 65-19672

Design Consultant: Milton Glaser
Type set by Graphic Arts Typographers Inc.
Printed by New York Lithographing Corp.
Bound by Publishers Book Bindery Inc.
Published by Reinhold Publishing Corporation
430 Park Avenue, New York, N. Y.

CONTENTS

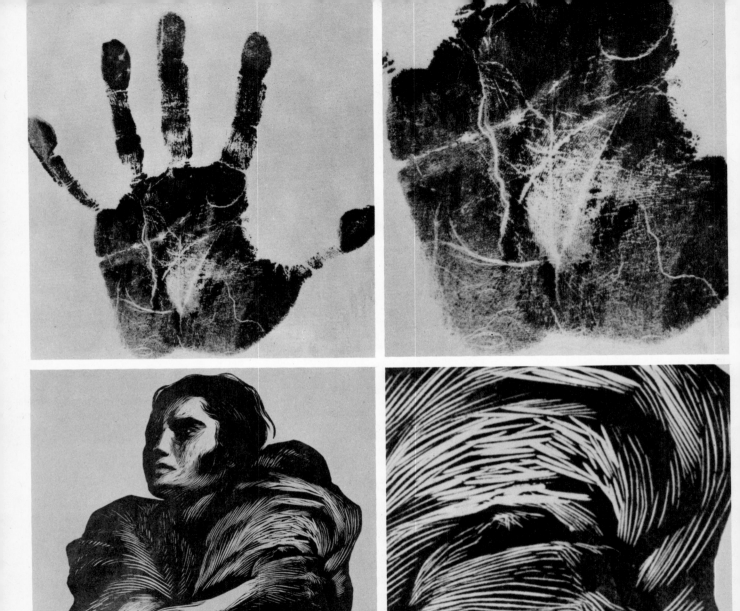

Linoleum print. Unknown Mexican Artist.

6

Introduction

A print is an impression made by an object on the surface of another object. Archaeological finds all over the world indicate that men in very early times used baked clay, wood, or metal stamps to press designs in damp clay, leather, and soft metals like gold and silver. Printing probably began when someone discovered that such a stamp could be dipped in color and lightly pressed on an object to make a design that would not be embossed *into* the surface, but remain "printed" *on top* of it. This was a very useful discovery. It increased the range of objects that could bear impressions to include fabrics and other materials too delicate or otherwise unsuitable for embossing. It also permitted more variety in design, for the same stamp could be used with numerous colors. The idea of being able to reproduce over and over again a motif, a number, a letter, or a picture grew into the exciting print making techniques we know today. These techniques and their applications are still growing.

In our times, inexpensive, readily available new materials that are easy to use allow print making to serve many purposes for many different people. Teachers use the simpler techniques to demonstrate how a single shape can be repeated to build up rich and intricate patterns. Amateur craftsmen make decorative prints on fabric for all sorts of purposes.

Artists, particularly younger artists, find print making a means for getting their ideas across in original form to a large public. Because many impressions can be made of each print, a single one can be purchased for a small price, even though each impression taken by an artist from his block is considered an original and is signed by him to indicate that he is satisfied with it.

Although a print can be a work of art, the process of print making is a craft, and there are many different ways to go about making a print. The materials the print maker has available to him, the size he wants his print to be, his knowledge of and experience in using tools, as well as the idea he wants to express, all enter into his choice of technique. Wood, linoleum, plaster, paper, clay, cardboard, Masonite, Plexiglas, metals of all kinds, fabrics and other "unlikely" materials have all been used to make blocks from which impressions have been printed.

Making a print need not be difficult or particularly complicated; some simple ways are described in the beginning of this book. Generally these ways involve making decorative shapes and repeating them, or finding objects that are interesting and printing them in a variety of ways.

More complex than finding or designing a shape and repeating it is making a block that will bear an original, highly personal idea. This involves intelligent planning and a certain amount of skill. One of the most satisfying aspects of print making is that translating an idea into a block encourages clear expression of that idea. Experimentation will reveal that the discipline of working with tools in a more or less resistent material forces formal relationships to emerge from what, on paper, might be merely random scribbles. A line that has been gouged out of wood or linoleum, or scratched on metal, or even dribbled as glue on cardboard, achieves at least a minimum of authority in translation. The evolving image can be worked over, around, under, or into with texture, line, and eventually color. The printed image may be strengthened by stencils, overprints, repetition, or by any other means that can be devised to make the final print as moving, powerful, dramatic, amusing, whimsical—as completely expressive—as possible.

The separate steps that are part of print making challenge the maker of a print to enlarge his skill in manipulating the physical materials from which he must fabricate his block, and also his skill in using the visual vocabulary of lines, forms, texture and colors as he attempts to create a work of art.

JANET ERICKSON
ADELAIDE SPROUL

1

Basic Printing Techniques

The simple series of activities in this chapter was designed to develop a feeling for the rhythmical progression of ideas and skills in print making. If you have never made a woodcut, a linoleum print or any other kind of print, we suggest you start here. If you are a teacher of art, we suggest you start others here. These beginning exercises are no more than a way of gaining confidence in print making techniques and establishing a feeling for what can be done with these techniques. They are a framework, a basis for further experimentation on one's own.

Most of us know that almost anything can be used to print. The dirty mark left by a child's hand on a clean wall and the impression of a tire in snow are kinds of prints. We also know that some prints last longer than others. Snow melts and the impression is gone. The child's hand print remains on the wall until it is washed off. This illustrates one of the basic considerations in print making— the need to make an indelible image.

Open a stamp pad and make your first indelible print—your own fingerprints (1). They have form and texture. What other familiar objects that have form and texture would you like to see printed? A coin can be pressed on the stamp pad and its pattern transferred to paper (2). In the resulting image you can clearly see one of the important characteristics of print making—the printed image is the mirror image of the original.

Rope can be twisted on the stamp pad and pressed onto the paper (3). That part in direct contact with the paper prints

4

3

5

better than those parts which only lightly touch it. This illustrates another consideration in print making—the image to be transferred must be brought into direct, firm contact with the surface which will bear the final print.

Look for other objects to print. A slice of onion from the kitchen can be inked with the stamp pad (4). The texture and shape of the print are pleasing but difficult to distinguish. Juice from the onion has diluted the stamp-pad ink. It is clear that ink strong in color and of good consistency is needed.

The onion is printed again, this time with printer's ink (5). The ink was spread over a nonabsorbent surface (a palette of Masonite or glass) and the onion pressed in it. The print is bolder and clearer due to the thickness and richness of pigment typical of printer's ink.

A fern was laid on the inked palette and gently pressed; then it was transferred, inked-side-down, to the paper and again pressed. The feathery quality of the leaf contrasts nicely with the sturdy character of the stem (6). If the fern had slipped on the paper, the print would have been muddy and blurred. A firm, steady approach is necessary in printing.

Half of a green pepper prints still another kind of form—a dark mass enclosed by heavy, irregular lines (7). The intervening space is sporadically interrupted by the marks of the seeds. Here we see how variation in the width and direction of lines can add to the interest of a print.

A piece of driftwood was pressed on the ink. Because of its roughness, only a few grains picked up the ink and the print was so poor we haven't bothered to reproduce it. Thus we have learned that laying an object in ink is not the most effective way of getting that object inked. It might be better to put ink *on* the object.

6

7

8

A tool is needed to transfer ink from the palette to the object. Fingers are useful, but this gets messy. Besides, clean fingers are needed for handling paper and for other print making operations. We improvised a simple tool by stuffing a soft rag into the toe of an old clean sock. A string was tied around the stuffed toe to make a small, soft ball. The resulting tool makes the excellent printer's device called a "pounce." We used a pounce to pat ink over the wood surface, and the resulting print (8) is strong and sharp.

A pounce is fine for inking small or very irregular surfaces. To spread ink evenly over a large, flat surface, however, a printer's brayer is a more effective tool. A brayer is a soft roller mounted in a handle. It helps control the amount and consistency of ink on the object to be printed. A thin film of ink is ideal. By spreading the ink over the palette and rolling it back and forth with the brayer, you can work it into a thin film. This film may be transferred with the brayer onto another piece of driftwood, or an onion half, or a green pepper. Or, perhaps you have a delicate object you wish to print. When printing delicate objects, like the bird's nest pictured here (9), you may prefer to press them directly onto your thinly inked palette. Notice the difference between the two prints of the bird's nest. The first print (a) is very delicate and intricately beautiful. The second (b) is more blurred and heavy looking. The pressure of printing pushed the delicate grasses together and the ink adhered them. Because a print maker usually wishes to make more than one impression, we have arrived at another consideration: A sturdy relief that can stand up under repeated printings is desirable.

This amusing print (10) was made from two sturdy objects that can be inked innumerable times and give a strong, sharp impression each time. The small piece of wood was inked with a brayer. The plastic toy wheel used for the eyes was inked with a pounce.

The plastic wheel was fun to use, so it was combined with a feather (11). The feather was laid in the ink, pressed to pick up an even film, then laid, inked-side-down, on paper. A piece of scrap paper was laid over the feather and a clean brayer used to roll gently and evenly.

9

a b

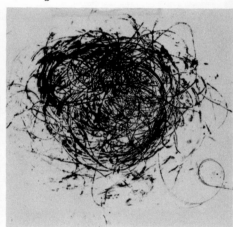

10

11

13

A slice of pumpernickel bread and part of an expansion watch band were inked with a brayer and printed (12). Almost any object can be inked by one means or another and printed. These prints are often interesting and amusing, but after you have enjoyed the decorative whimsey of a slice of pumpernickel and a piece of watch band turned into a pert animal, where do you go? Perhaps by making a whole row of pumpernickel-watch-band animals you could arrive at a pattern suitable for, say, a textile design. Playing around with natural objects, however, has its limitations because it is very difficult to divorce them from their identity. An artist needs tools and materials that he can manipulate to serve the idea he wants to express. This idea is the culminating point of experience, emotion, intellect, and intuition. It is the integrated product of several closely controlled factors, not a happy accident suggested by an "interesting" found object.

The print maker begins from scratch. He gathers together a simple set of basic tools: paper, ink, and materials for making an image or design in relief. He knows what you now know—that print making involves transferring an image. The more efficiently this is done, the better the print is technically. Technical skill, however, is not art. Where, then, does art come into the print making process? The answer is obvious—in creating an image and translating it into a form suitable for printing—a relief.

Working out an idea in relief is a large part of the print making process. To translate his idea into a relief, the print maker can cut into anything strong enough to endure repeated printing, or he may choose to glue shapes onto any firm ground. Most print makers prefer cutting out their relief. This may be a relatively simple process; for example, the image pictured here (13) was translated into a relief by incising lines in the flattened surface of a ball of plasticene. Another artist might have chosen to cut his idea into a piece of linoleum, a block of wood, Plexiglas, or paraffin. Any of these materials is suitable; they may all be easily worked by the artist into a vehicle for expressing his ideas through print making.

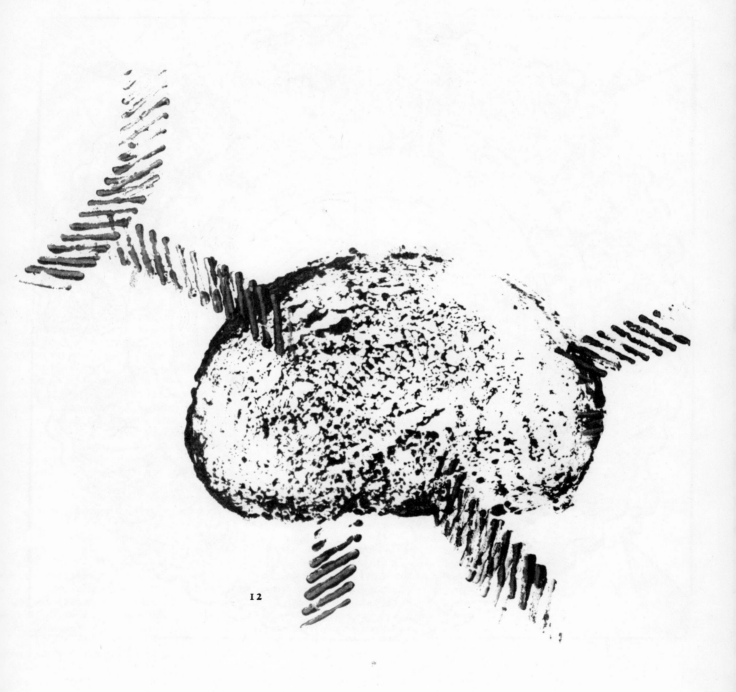

12

13

2

Printing With a Single Block—The Woodcut

Woodcuts have played a major role in the history of graphic art. The oldest prints were made from wood, and wooden relief blocks were used over a thousand years ago to print designs on textiles.

The history of woodcuts is closely allied to that of printing, and this has had a great influence on the quality of woodcuts as art. Before the invention of printing processes, the most common means of communication was word of mouth. Written documents were rare, simply because most people could not read or write. For those who could read, few books were available because books were made entirely by hand. The artist expressed himself by means appropriate to the times. He illuminated manuscripts, painted tableaus, wove tapestries, or sculpted.

Around 1400, various methods of printing were invented and books became more widely circulated. Then, as now, one picture was worth a thousand words, and a means of illustrating these books was needed. Hand drawing and painting could no longer be done on a scale adequate to supply the demand, so a faster and better means of providing multiple illustrations was needed. It is not difficult to imagine from where the idea came. The first type was cut from wood blocks, and low relief sculpture had been cut in wood for hundreds of years.

As books became available, more people learned to read and write. The demand for books and other printed materials increased. And the demand for illustrations grew. Subject matter expanded, and woodcuts were made to convey the kinds of information that blueprints, industrial photographs, technical renderings, and newspaper photographs serve today. Printing became an industry, and specialization developed.

Probably the first woodcuts were designed and cut by artists. Later, to keep up with the demand, artists designed the illustrations and craftsmen in the print shop cut them into reliefs for reproduction. Many of the master artists whose woodcuts are famous today seldom cut their own blocks.

Making woodcuts passed out of the hands of artists and into the hands of craftsmen. This had an effect on the quality of the illustration. Some craftsmen, of course, were quite skillful and could beautifully interpret drawings in wood. Others just cut wood.

Metal type replaced wooden type, and metal plates replaced wood blocks. Working with metal had several advantages. Instead of hewing a relief in wood, the craftsman could simply scratch a design. Also, with greater ease he could create tone with burnishing and etching techniques. Metal plates thus became the most important vehicles for graphic communication.

By the middle of the nineteenth century, however, wood blocks were once again in universal use, this time in the form of wood engraving. The earliest woodcuts were made from planks of wood. This meant that the craftsman had to deal with the grain of the wood and to cut a fairly high relief to get a clear print. But by using polished cross-cut sections of wood, the craftsman could engrave with the same ease as on metal plates. Cross-cut wood was much cheaper than metal plates. In addition, several pieces could be glued together to make large plates, or a piece could be cut apart and distributed to several craftsmen for engraving. At this point, woodcuts reached their nadir as works of art.

Printing and graphics had become the big business of publishing. Upon receiving a drawing or watercolor sketch an editor would send it directly to the "art department." Here the subject would be transferred to a wood block, which was then cut up like a jigsaw puzzle. The figures in the foreground would be assigned to one craftsman for cutting, those in the background to another, and the landscape areas to a third. Highly skilled, these men had to work quickly so

Since the wood block was the only means of printing illustrations, woodcuts served a wide variety of purposes. This early Italian Renaissance woodcut is an architectural rendering.

undesirable, it can easily be removed. Naturally, wood grain is not the prime consideration in creating an image in relief. Ease of carving is also important. Wood, even the hardest of woods, can be easy to work in. A sharp pencil drawn across the surface will leave a scratch deep enough to show up in the final print. These are technical considerations, of course, but the responsiveness of a medium is allied to the artist's joy in using it.

Most prints made from wood reliefs have a severe and powerful character. This is an outgrowth of working on the wood block itself. Wood is a no nonsense material. Tools must be kept sharp, and handled carefully. A bold approach can produce a print that is likewise bold and powerful, like the strong, definite strokes of the cutting tool. Handled differently, wood can also be cut with delicacy to print fine lines and tone through line.

The following section is limited to a description of the processes involved in making a print from a single wood block. Later sections will describe how this basic process can be elaborated to make multicolor prints from many blocks.

that the finished pieces could be reassembled, and the print published while it was still topical. In many of these illustrations the various styles of the several craftsmen who worked on them can easily be distinguished.

Making woodcuts conceived and executed solely as "art" is a fairly recent development. After photomechanical processes freed woodcuts from being the cheapest and easiest reproductive technique, artists seriously began to re-examine wood as a graphic art medium. The linear quality of wood grain is attractive; it can become an essential element in a print. Or, if the texture is

The Manner of the KING's TRYAL at *Westminster-hall*, by the High Court of Justice;

From January the 24th. to January the 27th. 1648. Also the Manner of His being put to Death at *White-hall*, near the Banquetting-house, on the 30th Day of January 1648; with His SPEECH made upon the Scaffold before He was Beheaded. To the Tune of, *Aim not too high, &c.*

King Charles was once a Prince of a great state,
But yet he dy'd a Death unfortunate;
Oh he is gone, and now hath I it is here
And God knows what courses we shall steer.

Now my sad Story to you I'll Relate.
At Westminster was call'd a Court of State,
Where Serjeant Bradshaw was Lord President,
The Court being sett, then in the King they sent.

The KING's Charge.

Charles Stuart, once admir'd in England's King,
Which did seek to turn upon the Kingdom bring,
In setting up the Standard in the Field,
Which was the cause that so much Blood was Spilt.

Whereas thou didst Raise Arms within the Land,
Against us and the Parliament did withstand:
The People's Rights and Liberties contrary,
And rose and rere thou didst Tyrannical.

Therefore you Guilty are of these sad times,
As People, Murder, and all such like Crimes;
Now which is that is still our purpose,
And in this Court you shall have a Tryal fair.

Here is your Jury, for to judge thee so,
You've heard your Charge, Found Guilty, Aye, or no.

When it was done, then answered the King,
How is for this you did me hither bring?

The King's Answer to the Charge.

As for your Charge a Rush I do not care,
I do ceste thou's bringus a wright and square;
It may be my fraght's breed as I am found,
The Liberties and Laws of all the Land.

I did fee to me you would so sold,
By way of Commission you this Court do hold,
To whom the President did fit right Reply,
Sir you shall own by whole Authority.

This Court-Prerogative where in we stand,
Ordain'd us by the Commons of this Land;
It is not for Prisoners to difpute the same:
Answer to that for which you hither come.

Then their Authority he quite Deny'd,
And said by them he meant not to be Try'd.
At which the Court their Verdict then did pass,
Not withstanding, that he then Guilty was.

Then by the Clerk his Sentence there was Read,
Saying, Charles Stuart, Thou must lose thy Head
For Murther, Treason, and for Tyranny,
And to the Land a publick Enemy.

Being Condemned one thing he did Crave,
That Children's Rights to Preface he might have,
To Preach, and his Communion Him to give;
And for His own poor Babes which He did Live;

The which was Granted, all Perform'd and done,
And he did see his Daughter and his Son:
It would have Griev'd a Stony Heart to see
The weeping Joy that was between those Three.

He blest them both, and for them he did Pray,
Mourning at Parting, then they go their way,
Father from Children, 'twas a Grief full fore,
Each other in this World to fee no more.

Thus on the Thirteenth of January last,
He from St. James's unto White-Hall past;
Having a Guard of flying Colours spread,
And Rattling Drums as he Marched led.

With cheerful Countenance and Courage Bold,
He said, Marek Fafter, for the Day is Cold,
Then to the Scaffold he was straight Convey'd,
The which with Mourning Cloath was overlaid.

The King's Speech upon the Scaffold.

Mounting the same, quoth he, I'll little say,
For in this World I have not long to stay:
It is my Duty first with God to over,
My Conscience free, next to my Country Dear:

Unto the Parliament I never thought ill,
Their Priviledges never thought to spill;
Ill Instruments on both fides bred the Strife,
Which was the cause so many lost their Life.
The great'st Enemies that fought my Death,
I do forgive, before I lose my Breath.

I wish the Kingdoms Peace and Charles's Bliss,
For now Religion out of Order is;
Lawful Succession I do hope shall be,
Granted by Parliament now after me:
And for my Confcience and Religion,
I dye a Protestant and a Christian.

To Doctor Juxon then his George he gave,
Willing Prince Charles his Son the fame might have,
His walking Staff unto himself did give,
And for his fake to keep whilft he did live.
Likewise he gave the Duke of Richmond then
One Watch, another to a Gentleman;
With Eyes lift up to Heaven he made a Prayer,
And then for Death did instantly prepare.

Saying, My Earthly Crown I here muft leave,
Hoping a Heavenly Crown I shall receive,
Then on the Block his Neck there he did lay,
And to the Headman then thefe Words did fay,
When as my Hands and Arms I open stretch,
Strike Home, before that thou a wight Blow fetch,
Jesus, I come Lord Jesus, then he cry'd,
One Blow his head and Body did Devide.

Thus like a Lamb his Death ha there did take,
And presently this World he did forfake:
Whole Soul I truft is with the Lord on high,
And thus I end my Mournful Tragedy.

Printed by and for C. B. and sold by J. Walter.

The King's Tryal, English broadside, 17th century. (Courtesy the Fogg Museum, Cambridge, Mass.)

A flurry of broadsides was issued after noteworthy events. This one concerns the trial of King Charles, who was beheaded in 1648 during the Reformation in England. The words recount the trial and beheading, and are to be sung— so the Broadside says—to the tune of "Aim not too high &c."

Bottom

The Pope (Clement XIII) Receiving a Messenger by Jean Michel Papillon (1698-1776). (Courtesy The Cooper Union Museum, New York.)

This wood block shows the high degree of artistry that several woodcutters attained. The block, done in France about 1765, portrays the Pope and messenger in intricate detail, a crowd of onlookers, and a view of St. Peter's Square, at the left.

THE

ELEPHANT,

ACCORDING to the account of the celebrated BUFFON, is the most respectable Animal in the world. In size he surpasses all other terrestrial creatures; and by his intelligence, makes as near an approach to man, as matter can approach spirit. A sufficient proof that there is not too much said of the knowledge of this animal is, that the Proprietor having been absent for ten weeks, the moment he arrived at the door of his apartment, and spoke to the keeper, the animal's knowledge was beyond any doubt confirmed by the cries he uttered forth, till his Friend came within reach of his trunk, with which he caressed him, to the astonishment of all those who saw him. This most curious and surprising animal is just arrived in this town, from Philadelphia, where he will stay but a few days.———He is only four years old, and weighs about 3000 weight, but will not have come to his full growth till he shall be between 30 and 40 years old. He measures from the end of his trunk to the tip of his tail 15 feet 8 inches, round the body 10 feet 6 inches, round his head 7 feet 2 inches, round his leg above the knee 3 feet 3 inches, round his ankle 2 feet 2 inches. He eats 130 weight a day, and drinks all kinds of spirituous liquors; some days he has drank 30 bottles of porter, drawing the corks with his trunk. He is so tame that he travels loose, and has never attempted to hurt any one. He appeared on the stage, at the New Theatre in Philadelphia, to the great satisfaction of a respectable audience.

A respectable and convenient place is fitted up adjoining the Store of Mr. Bartlet, Market-Street, for the reception of those ladies and gentlemen who may be pleased to view the greatest natural curiosity ever presented to the curious, which is to be seen from sunrise till sundown, every day in the week.

☞ The Elephant having destroyed many papers of consequence, it is recommended to visitors not to come near him with such papers.

Admittance *ONE QUARTER OF A DOLLAR*——Children *ONE EIGHTH OF A DOL-LAR.*
NEWBURYPORT, Sept. 19, 1797.

The Elephant, American broadside, 1797. (Courtesy The New York Historical Society, New York City.)

Woodcuts were widely used for making broadsides, a kind of handbill that was distributed among the populace and posted in public places. This famous broadside announces the arrival of "the greatest natural curiosity ever presented to the curious." Although the broadside says the beast is friendly, it also warns those carrying "papers of consequence" not to bring them near him.

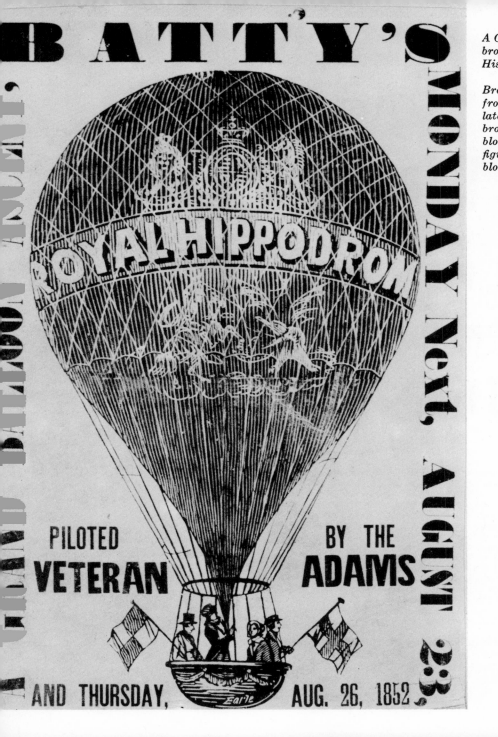

A Grand Balloon Assent, American broadside, 1852. (Courtesy The New York Historical Society, New York City.)

Broadsides announced numerous things, from weekly grain prices to the latest daring feats. This particular broadside was made from more than one block. One basic block contained the figures and balloon; other interchangeable blocks bore various dates.

Bandbox, 19th century American. (Courtesy The Cooper Union Museum, New York.)

Woodcuts served decorative as well as illustrative purposes. This particular one enhances a hatbox and effectively labels its contents.

Independent Greenback Party, American.
(Courtesy The Cooper Union Museum,
New York.)

There was a woodcut for almost every
purpose. This one, a wood engraving, is a
political notice. Wood engraving
techniques made possible the mass
production of graphic art, frequently to
the detriment of its esthetic content.
Notice how mechanically rendered are the
clothes and background in the portrait.

The Garroter's Reward—A Scene in
Newgate, illustration from Harper's
Weekly, 1872.

In order to publish an illustration while it
was still news, it was common practice
to cut up a wood block and distribute the
pieces to various craftsmen for engraving.
By examining the print, you can
distinguish how it was cut. The five figures
at left front were cut by a craftsman
who had considerable artistic ability as
well as technical skill.

Creating an image. We have described print making as unique among art forms because a large part of the final result must be created on the block. The artist is working, by stages that rely on a number of techniques, toward an image that will stand as a work of art. Most artists work out what they have in mind by drawing it beforehand on a sheet of paper or directly on the block. Some experienced print makers, however, feel they can achieve fresh, spontaneous effects by freely cutting the image in the wood with a minimum of advance drawing.

If you do start by making a drawing for a woodcut, remember that the lines of the drawing cannot be exactly reproduced by the cutting tools. Work out your idea by drawing it a number of ways, if necessary, and then letting the lines on the block serve simply as guides for interpreting the design in the spirit of the material and the tools. Remember also that the image will be reversed in the print; this is particularly important when lettering is involved. It is a good idea to draw the final version of the design on a piece of paper in compressed charcoal, which makes a soft, dusty line. Lay the drawing *face down* on the block and gently rub it. The charcoal transfers easily, and the design will be reversed. As a result, the printed image will be going in the same direction as the original drawing. Strengthen the faint charcoal lines with brush and ink so they will not rub away as you cut. When drawing directly on the block, always use charcoal or India ink; even soft pencil lines can scratch and scar the surface of the block.

Cutting the wood block. When the drawing is fairly clearly indicated it is time to start cutting away all the parts that are not to print. Once an area is removed it can receive no ink and transfer none to the paper. In other words, a cut area leaves a white space. Sharp tools are essential. No matter how "soft" the wood is, it is none the less wood and relatively hard. Dull tools tear the wood and are dangerous and frustrating to use because they are difficult to control. Always turn

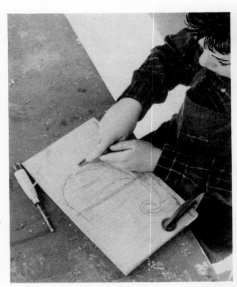

1. *Print making is exciting to people of all ages, and anyone can make a woodcut, even a young child. The basic processes are simple and fun. This child drew directly on his wood block. Since his design is simple and no lettering is involved, this approach is quite adequate. He has clamped the block to the work table, and is now cutting it. Note that he is working with the sharp point of the gouge away from his body. When he wants to change the direction of his cutting, he will unfasten the block and reposition it so that he is always cutting away from himself.*

2. *The child is rolling the brayer on the block with smooth, flowing strokes. He wi ink it in all directions in case the block is slightly warped, and apply ink until the block is shiny. Notice that only those part in high relief receive the ink.*

3. Having laid a sheet of paper slightly larger than the block over the block, the child is rubbing it with a smooth metal spoon. He will rub with small circular motions until the paper under the spoon darkens. This means the ink has transferred.

4. The print has been pulled off the block, and the young artist is appraising it. He may like it as it is, or choose to cut some more, or decide he prefers another color or another kind of paper. Whatever his decision, he has become a print maker.

the block so the sharp end of the tool is being pushed away from you. Tools can, and do, slip.

Since you will be exerting a great deal of pressure, the block may slip out from under the tool unless it is secured. C-clamps can be used to fasten the block to a table or work bench but may mar the wood unless padded. A helpful solution is the simple device known as a stop block, illustrated under " glossary " at the end of the book.

The first cuts need not be deep. It is unnecessary and usually wrong to angle a tool so that it cuts straight down into the block; this may cause splintering. You should gradually work away the wood to reveal the image. Hold the tool at about the angle you would hold a pencil and try a cut. If the wood is too resistant, reduce the angle until cutting is easier. Experiment with the less essential parts of your design, as a few mistakes in the peripheral areas are not disastrous. Experiment with the tools. Generally you will find gouges ideal for cutting along the grain of wood, a straight knife will make a cleaner cut across the grain.

Making a proof. As soon as the image is roughly cut, it is time to make the first proof. A proof is a print taken from an unfinished block. This is a very important step because it allows you to judge the progress of your idea. Is the image clear? Will cutting away more wood clarify the design and make it "read" as you had planned? Often a proof reveals unexpected qualities in the rough cutting which bring out new and exciting possibilities. Don't be afraid to incorporate these happy accidents into the design. They will become part of your personal vocabulary with experience. It is helpful, when you are not sure of your next step, to work it out on the proof. Use opaque white paint over uncut areas to judge the effect of more cutting.

It is important to take a proof early in the cutting process because the interplay of lights and darks on the relief itself is often misleading. One of the delights of print making is that once the block is cut, nothing you do in the printing process can radically change it. The basic design remains no matter how much you elaborate by using stencil overlays, changing colors, or experimenting with exotic papers.

Inking the block. To make a proof, the block must be inked. Roll an even coat of ink onto the brayer and roll the inked brayer lightly over the block. Only those areas in high relief will take the ink. The block has received enough ink when the surfaces appear shiny. Roll the brayer over the block in several directions because wood is often slightly warped and the brayer tends to skip over any unevenness. Wood is apt to absorb a considerable amount of ink the first time it is used, so it may be necessary to go over the block a number of times before the pattern looks shiny. If the brayer is rigid and hard it will not ink even the slightest depressions in the block. A soft brayer is a much more sensitive tool and should be used if at all possible.

Transferring the image. Newsprint is adequate for making a proof. Cut a piece of paper an inch or so larger than the block and gently lay it over the inky surface, smoothing it out from the center somewhat the way you smooth a table cloth. This helps avoid wrinkling and spreads the paper evenly over the block. You now need pressure to transfer the ink from block to paper. For this you need a tool to rub the paper. The tool you choose will greatly influence the quality of the print. Many people use the back of a smooth wooden or metal spoon, as this makes a clear, definite, dark print. Your hand or an old soft piece of leather stretched over wood or folded securely (old bill-folds are ideal) will make a more sensitive impression. The Japanese use a bamboo leaf stretched around a piece of cardboard.

Hold the rubbing implement firmly and start in the center of the paper, rubbing with a circular motion, working out to the edge in all directions. As the ink begins to transfer, the area under the implement will darken. When you have rubbed over the entire proof, pull back one corner and look at it. (The sticky ink will keep the rest of the paper from slipping at this stage.) If you feel the print should be darker and there is still ink left on the block, work the paper back into place and rub some more.

When the rubbing has been accomplished, pick the paper up carefully by one corner and slowly peel it off the block. The first view of your idea translated into bold black-and-white areas is always a surprise and often the image will seem to have become quite different from your original idea. Study this first proof carefully and become acquainted with it, then make plans for any further cutting needed to refine and clarify your idea.

Keep all the proofs you make. They provide a kind of visual growth chart of the print that shows where you have been and where you are going.

Making the print. The last phase of print making is making the finished print. Having finished cutting the block, you are almost ready to print a series of finished impressions. At this point there are a number of possibilities. The first concerns the type of paper to use and the kind and color of ink. Some papers are much more absorbent than others, and the surface on which you choose to print is determined by the character (fine line or bold and coarse) of the relief block. Experiment with any available papers, and while doing this also experiment with color if this is not to be a black-and-white block. As you have worked with your proofs, other decisions probably have been made concerning how you rub the ink onto the paper and which areas, if any, should be treated in a special way.

Anyone who has ever used a simple block to create a series of prints knows that all kinds of variables operate in the printing process. Your finished prints will not be exactly identical, and this is as it should be. This is what it means to print by hand, without the mechanical help of a press. No matter how controlled you are, some prints will be slightly lighter and some darker, some more sensitive and pleasing for subtle, hard-to-define reasons. Each print is different because you are, even when not fully aware of it, exercising creative judgment up to the very last moment before peeling the print from the block.

It's Me by a preschool child.
This amusing print by a small child was simply conceived and cut. Notice that the child cut out the lines he drew on the block, rather than cutting around them to leave them in high relief. He created a kind of negative portrait. The paper is colored construction paper; the wood is clear pine, which is easy to cut and excellent for boldly conceived images.

Portrait by a ninth grade student, Shady
Hill School, Cambridge, Mass.
This self-portrait is quite sophisticated.
The boy cut around the lines he drew on
the block to put them in high relief. This
produces a black-on-white print. The wood
grain in the hair and clothes is descriptive.

Opposite page
Three-block color woodcut by Fay
Eisenman. Soft pine blocks, hand-rubbed
print on Troya rice paper. (Reproduced
by permission of the Printmaking classes
of the High School of Music and Art,
New York City.)

At the Table by Louis Valtat. (Collection The Museum of Modern Art, New York. Gift of Peter Deutsch.)

Here mass is contrasted with mass. There is freely cut stark white against deep black with no gradation of tone. The linear quality of wood grain, so often evident in woodcuts, has been completely underplayed in this brooding portrait.

Opposite page
Sunset in the Mountains by Lyonel Feininger, 1918. (Collection The Museum of Modern Art, New York. Gift of the artist and his wife.)

The mature print maker plans ahead. Here the artist has created two kinds of visual and emotional impressions. The black-on-white buildings on top of the mountain are in full, almost glaring, light The white-on-black structures on the mountainside seem to be fleetingly picked out of sombre shadows by the last rays of the sun.

L'ARGENT

*L'Argent by Felix Vallotton. (Collection
The Museum of Modern Art, New York.
Gift of Abby Aldrich Rockefeller.)*

*The large area of black in this woodcut
theatrically focuses attention on the small,
but emphatic white figures.*

The Alchemists by Arthur Deshaies, 1953.
(Collection The Museum of Modern Art,
New York.)

An almost calligraphic black line has
been achieved in this wood engraving by
boldly cutting away areas of white. The
gray tones were made by repeated cuts
with a fine scribe.

Opposite page

The Wave by Aristide Maillol, 1895.
(Collection The Museum of Modern Art,
New York. Gift of Mrs. Donald B. Straus.)

The simple white figure in this print seems
almost sculptural when contrasted with
the stylized turbulence of the water. Note
how the flow of the hair has been
differentiated from that of the water by
using finer lines cut in a different
direction.

Lion by Howard Burns, 1965.

In this wood engraving the artist has beautifully revived some formerly common
techniques that are not often used today. Much of the cutting was done with special tools.
The body, for example, was done with a tool that makes indentations in the wood.

Above
Death Before an Open Grave, Anonymous German, c. 1470-80. (Courtesy Museum of Fine Arts, Boston.)

This is a hand colored woodcut from a book. Sometimes the coloring was done at the print shop, but often it was commissioned or done later by the proud owners of the book. The quality of coloring varied greatly, and some woodcuts were even gilded.

Right
Lady in the Middle Ages by Bernard Reder, 1949. (Collection The Museum of Modern Art, New York. Abby Aldrich Rockefeller Fund.)

Several colors were rolled, wiped, and brushed onto this single block to define and enhance the volumes. A variety of inking styles may be seen in the hat.

Top left
After an Iran Sculpture by John Bernhardt, 1956. (Courtesy The Print Council of America, New York.)

The abstract quality in this handsome print of a lion dragging down a bull is emphasized by the great amount of purely decorative surface detail.

Bottom left
Berkshire Trees by Adelaide Sproul.

These freely interpreted forms were inspired by watching the continually shifting relationships between light and dark in a forest. Irregularities in the pine plank continually reminded the artist of the quality of trees as she worked on the relief block.

Opposite page
Dancing by Raoul Dufy, 1912. (Collection The Museum of Modern Art, New York.)

In some parts of this woodcut the black and white areas are of almost equal size, making a lively tension between the white faces and hands of the dancing figures and the trees which surround them. The light triangle enclosing the black ship introduces deep space into an otherwise flat design.

LA DANSE

37

migdowsky:
cabbage in a de 1964

Top

The Barn Owl by Eric Daglish. (Courtesy Museum of Fine Arts, Boston.)

Using cross-cut sections of wood instead of planks permits the engraving of very fine lines. A wide variety of tones can be developed with fine lines; note especially the naturalistic quality of the feathers.

Bottom
Masks by Erich Heckel, 1907. (Collection The Museum of Modern Art, New York.)

Wood grain has a definite direction which influences many print makers. Here the artist has turned a physical quality into an esthetic consideration—the haunting feeling of the masks is emphasized by their angularity.

Opposite page
Cabbage by Jacques Hinzdovsky, 1964.

The lines in this print follow the form and direction of each leaf, yet they describe the cabbage as a whole. There is a complete range of tone from light to dark, yet the print was made on gray paper.

*Horseman II by Arthur Danto, 1956.
(Courtesy The Print Council of America,
New York City.)*

*This fluidly cut horse and rider seems
alive, quick, and spontaneous, yet the image
was cut in wood. Almost any feeling can
be developed in wood if the artist is
skillful enough.*

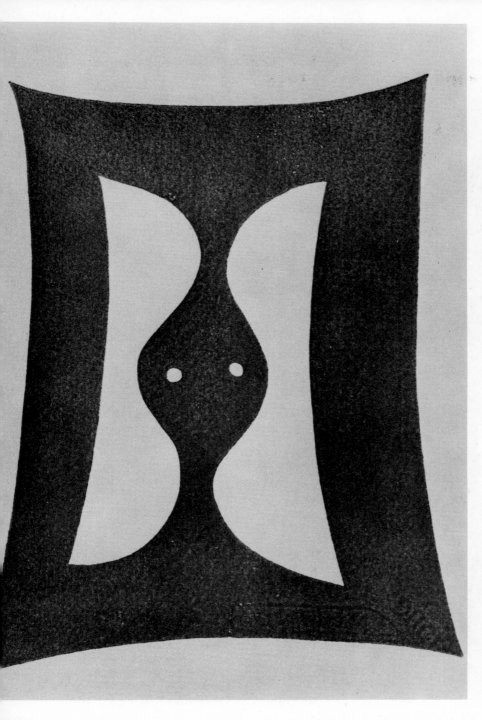

The Window of the Universe by Jean
(Hans) Arp. (Collection The Museum of
Modern Art, New York.)

A single block need not be printed only in
black; colored inks may also be used. Here
the ink was yellow. The completely flat
design becomes three dimensional as you
concentrate on it. The interior light areas
seem to pierce the dark shape and fall open
on to the universe.

The Last Hurrah by a student at Shady Hill School, Cambridge, Mass.

More than one color can be used on a single block. Here the inking was rather simple because the figure is clearly defined by a nimbus. The figure was printed in black, and the very lightly scored background in red.

The Waiters by a student at Shady Hill School, Cambridge, Mass., 1962.

Repeating one block in two colors is often quite effective. One horizontal band of repeated prints overlaps the second row of repeats, giving the print a gay, sidewalk cafe air.

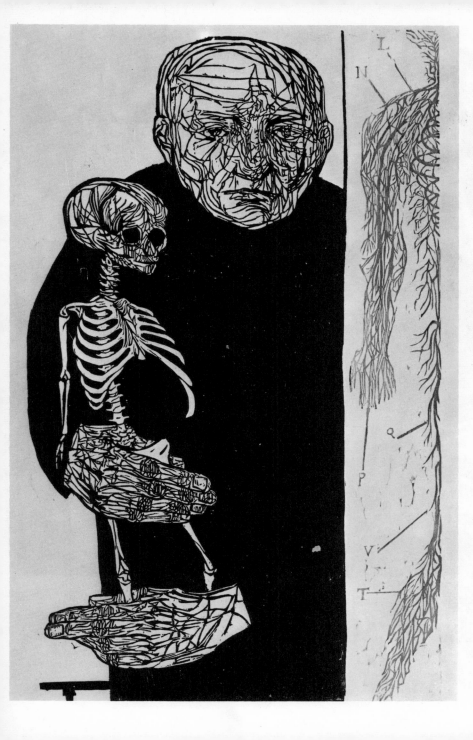

The Anatomist by Leonard Baskin, 1952.
(Collection The Museum of Modern Art,
New York. Gift of the Junior Council.)

The anatomical chart on the right side of
this print is red. The man was printed in
black, but note how the delicate tracery in
the hands, head, and skeleton affects his
flat, dark bulk.

Death as a Juggler by Christian Rohlfs. (Courtesy The Brooklyn Museum.)

Hand coloring of woodcuts is still practiced. The modern artist who cut and printed this block also painted it. Although a series of prints run from a single block is usually quite similar, hand coloring introduces quite a bit of variety.

Horses and Riders, Russian, 18th century. (Courtesy The Cooper Union Museum, New York City.)

Single blocks of wood were often printed in one color, then several colors of paint or dye were brushed into certain areas to enrich the design. On this old linen textile, an overall design was printed in one dye color, while another dye color was brushed here and there to add interest.

Fashion Plate, early 19th century, French. (Courtesy The Cooper Union Museum, New York City.)

The kind of information contained in a fashion plate hasn't changed much, just the style. Romance, spring, and all good things are promised milady, if only she will dress in the latest vogue.

Barking Dog by Shiko Munakata, 1959.
(Collection The Museum of Modern Art,
New York.)

Calligraphy is often successfully combined
with images from nature. This woodcut,
whose design relies almost entirely on a
cut-away pattern, was printed from a
single block in one color.

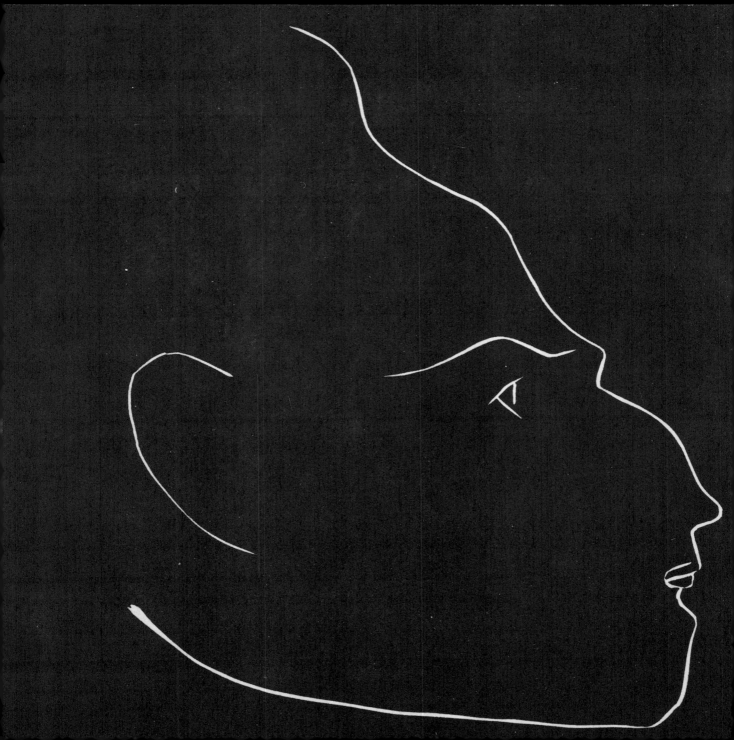

3

Printing With a Single Block—The Linoleum Print

A print made from a linoleum block may have the bold contrast of unrelieved black and white areas, or subtle tonal gradations of great delicacy. The linoleum used in print making is flexible and fairly soft, and is therefore easy to cut. It is smooth, with little texture of its own, but this soft surface can be gouged, poked, carved, skived and otherwise manipulated in an almost infinite variety of ways to make textures from which impressions can be taken. There is no grain, so lines can be cut across and around, up and down and through the surface in any direction. This makes linoleum a sympathetic medium in which to execute freely flowing designs. Because linoleum is so easy to handle, you can approach the construction of a block in several different ways. The method you choose will depend somewhat on the size of the print, as well as on the general effect you hope to achieve.

Designing a linoleum print. Linoleum is a wonderful material for experimentation. You may decide to design an entire print on a single piece of linoleum, or choose to make motifs that may be repeated in several different ways. The latter approach is almost painterly in concept— you create the overall design as you print.

Cutting a linoleum block. You can use almost any kind of sharp knife or gouge to carve a design into the surface of a linoleum block; to take advantage of the full range of possibilities of this malleable material you should try many different cutting tools. You should have at least one narrow, deep V-gouge, one wide, deep V-gouge, and one wide background scooper. *Always cut away from you,* and always keep the hand holding the linoleum behind the cutting point of the tool. Tools should be kept sharp. Dull tools slip and are more dangerous to use than sharp ones. Cut as deep down into the linoleum as you can. Shallow lines tend to fill up with ink after one or two impressions have been taken. It does no harm to cut down through the cloth backing of the linoleum. You may even want to cut some big background areas away entirely with scissors or a knife.

There are many different kinds of linoleum made by many different companies. Some, like "counter-top," are soft and easy to cut; other types, such as "battleship" and the rubber and vinyl tile products, are much harder and more resistant to the cutting tool. However, these hard linoleums are much easier to cut when slightly warm. Very little heat is needed. In the winter the heat from a warm radiator is sufficient; on a summer's day the heat from the sun will usually soften up the hardest, grittiest pieces of linoleum.

Backing the linoleum. Linoleum is rather thin. If a design is very linear or strung out or lacy, the linoleum will become floppy and hard to handle as the background areas are cut away. The linoleum for this kind of design should be mounted *before* you begin to cut your design out of it. Use heavy cardboard or Masonite for the backing, and fasten the linoleum to it with a quick-setting white casein glue. Large blocks (8″ by 10″ or larger) should be placed under weights until dry to prevent warping.

A design consisting mostly of solid areas can be mounted after it has been cut. If there are any unnecessary background sections, these should be cut completely away with a scissors or knife before the linoleum is mounted. Any large areas of backing should be sealed and protected with shellac so that if ink is accidentally rolled, smeared, or dropped there it can be wiped off cleanly and easily. The back of the block can also be protected in this way. Also, it is helpful when printing to have some indication on the back of the block of where the principal parts of the pattern are located, or which is the top of the design.

Printing with a linoleum block. Linoleum

1. One of the most pleasant and popular motifs in design is the flower. Here a simple flower is being sketched directly on a piece of linoleum. White pencil is used for contrast. Poster paint or liquid white shoe polish can also be used, and they have the added advantage of being easy to wipe off if corrections are necessary.

blocks, even when mounted, are more flexible than wood blocks and can be printed best by pressing the inked surface down onto the paper or fabric. The material to be printed should be spread out flat on a smooth, well padded printing bed. (For instructions on preparing a printing bed, see "Technical Notes.") Where you lay your printing bed depends on the size of the print and how you choose to print it. The simplest way to print a block is to step onto the back of it; this, of course, means your printing bed should be on the floor. The bed could also be laid on a table top and the block printed by leaning on it, or by hitting it with a rubber mallet. Whatever your choice, make sure that you apply pressure to each section of the block if you want an even impression.

Linoleum blocks are durable, light and flexible and can be used over and over again. They are extremely practical for printing draperies, bed spreads, and other projects. The larger the block, of course, the fewer prints needed. When printing with really large blocks, or on long lengths of fabric for draperies or wall hangings, you should have a printing bed large enough to spread out and print the whole piece at one time. This makes it possible to plan the design in relation to the total length, allowing for proper hems and headings and, even more important, arranging the design so that it fits gracefully into the space it has to fill.

Designing with a motif block. Linoleum is a wonderful medium for experimenting with printed designs. The following section shows a few of the many things that can be done with a single, simple motif.

2. Once the motif is satisfactory, proceed with the cutting. The areas around the outline of this flower are being cut away so that the flower itself will print. Always keep in mind that the areas in high relief are those that will print. Again, notice how the artist is working the gouges away from the body. The hand holding the linoleum is also kept behind the gouge. When the linoleum has been cut, it will be glued on a block for easier handling.

3. Here is how the motif prints. By itself it is interesting. The flower fills the space well and the gouge lines left in the background frame the petals nicely. However pleasing the impression is, though, it is only a motif. What can be done with it?

4. A series of simple repeats is tried. The pointed petal shapes give a lively overall effect. However, the gouge lines in the background create new and somewhat distracting design elements between the juxtaposed flowers.

An open, checkerboard pattern is neater. To help align the impressions, squares of the same size as the block were cut out of cardboard. Using them saves a lot of tedious measuring and is frequently more accurate.

Opposite page
Top left: *Sliding the block down a half length each row creates a somewhat different, but rather disorganized, effect. This kind of design is called a half-drop repeat.*

Top right: *This more complex design is full of new relationships. The first simple repeat pattern has been overprinted in a darker tone with a second group of impressions printed half a length over and half a length down.*

Bottom left: *The pleasant variety of tones in this series comes from making several prints with the block before re-inking it. The effect is interesting and seems worth developing.*

Bottom right: *Here we have something. The eye is caught and moved over the pattern by the variations in tone between the motifs. The strongly linear texture of this new kind of paper, a Japanese rice paper, enhances the design. The pattern is satisfying and the print is beautiful.*

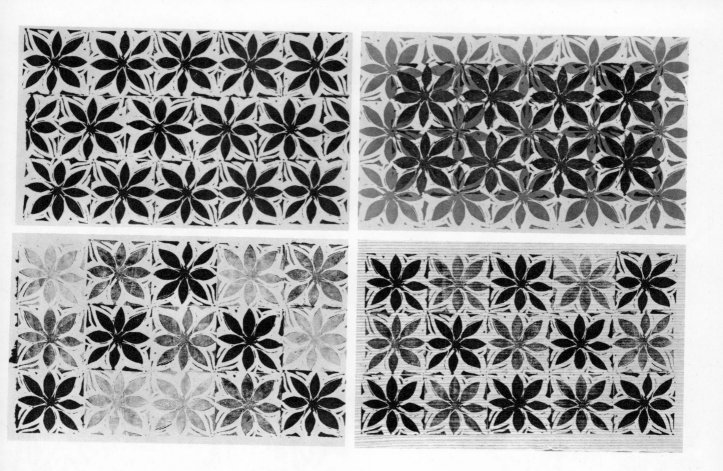

Floral Sprays by Janet Doub Erickson.

Count the number of times only one block was used. The darkest tone is bright green. The two lighter tones were made by printing an inked block twice. The result is a strong yellow and a faint yellow.

Textile Design by a Junior High School student, Worcester, Mass.

When a simple motif is printed in alternating red and blue, a lively surface decoration can result. All impressions, except that in dead center, face the same direction.

Fabric Design by Roberta Klug.

Three small linoleum blocks with simple designs have been repeated in a random fashion to create this intricate, allover pattern.

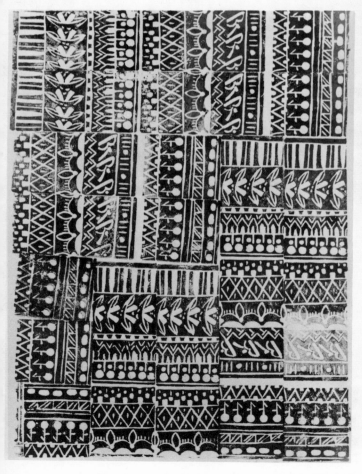

Broadside by Janet Doub Erickson.

Here is a linoleum block beside its print, which is white on red. Since a print is a mirror image of the block, the letters are reversed on the block. The easiest and most accurate way to get letters in reverse on a block is to letter the text roughly in pastels on a sheet of paper. Then place the paper face down on the block and rub the back of it. The dusty pastel will transfer to the block. Since the direction of the letters is now set down correctly, freely design each character as you cut it. The ease of cutting linoleum encourages this approach.

Opposite page
Car by a student of Shady Hill School,
Cambridge, Mass.

A fifth grade boy used a fine gouge directly
on the linoleum without previous drawing.
The result is fresh and spontaneous.

Moses by Joyce Bissell.

The simple direct lines cut with a wide,
deep gouge forcefully interpret this
massive head.

Top
Winter by a junior-high-school student, Worcester, Mass.

Printing this design in white on dark paper emphasizes the simplicity of an imaginative idea, boldly carried out.

Middle
Christmas Card by a student of Shady Hill School, Cambridge, Mass.

The reindeer, man, and snowflakes were cut with a single gouged line over lines drawn freely on the block. The print was made in white on green paper.

Bottom
Landscape by an elementary student at Kamehameha Schools, Honolulu, Hawaii.

Dots, short and long strokes, and widely spaced gouges were executed with a single tool—the wide gouge. The kind of mark in each area seems tactilely interpreted. The ground is hard and sandy; it is defined with jabs into the linoleum. The river running through the land to the sea and the sea itself were made with more flowing strokes:

Opposite page
Bird on a Nest by a student at Marshfield Junior High, Marshfield, Mass.

This broadly defined bird greets the morning sun, whose rays are indicated by the free cutting of the background.

Fall River From Across the Meadow by Anthony Lopes.

Lines can be cut with a great deal of variety. Here the broad strokes of the gouge left fine lines to relieve the large white areas. Note how the lines grow up from the black border of the print.

Emblem by a student of Marshfield Junior High School, Marshfield, Mass.

The big, bold letters are patriotic in concept.

Seated Nude, Arms Crossed by Henri Matisse, 1906. (Collection The Museum of Modern Art, New York. Abby Aldrich Rockefeller Fund.)

A wide gouge was used almost like a broad brush. The cutting is loose and free.

Frontispiece by Henri Matisse. (Collection The Museum of Modern Art, New York. Gift of Abby Aldrich Rockefeller.)

Linoleum is appropriate for developing any idea. Matisse made a series of linoleum cuts as illustrations for Pasiphaé–Chant de Minos (Les Crétois) by Henry de Montherlant, published in 1944.

Hail, King by Carl G. Nelson.

The freely executed lines in the face, hair, and hands are emphasized by the contrast with the more rigidly cut lines in the background and by the large, dark areas.

Calaveras Estranguladoras by Alfredo Zalce and Leopoldo Mendez, 1942. (Collection The Museum of Modern Art, New York. Gift of Pablo O'Higgins.)

The surface of the linoleum has been scraped, scored, and cut with a fine engraving tool to make the grays in this powerful print. The lettering formed of parts of skeletons was also cut in linoleum.

Primitive Man by Max Weber, 1918(?).
(Collection The Museum of Modern Art,
New York. Gift of Abby Aldrich
Rockefeller.)

A single block was inked with black, flesh
tint, red, orange, and blue to get a
multicolor impression. The image was
probably transferred by rubbing paper
laid over the block with the hand.

Opposite page
Left: *Apple Picking by Doris Rockenbach.*

A single block was inked in two shades of
green to make this print. A third color, the
red of the apples, was touched in with the
eraser end of a pencil.

Right: *Death and the Child by Christian*
Rohlfs, 1912-1913. (Collection The
Museum of Modern Art, New York.
Matthew T. Mellon Foundation Fund.)

How pressure is applied to make ink
transfer from the block to paper can
affect the print. Here the block may have
been printed face down on a printing bed
composed of burlap or some other
textured material, or it may have been
printed face up using a rough tool to rub
it.

4

Printing With More Than One Block—The Color Print

Color provokes emotional responses. Color may have dynamic impact—the force of a bright red against black; or it may be subtle—the quiet nostalgia of light blues and greens. By itself color can stir and inspire; in a work of art it is an additional means of expressing an idea. Colors are the adjectives of visual language.

There are two basic ways to use color in print making. In the first approach color is decorative; it is added to enrich an already complete image. In the second color helps form the image.

Color prints may be made in several ways. Some involve inking more than one color directly on a single block and transferring all the colors in one printing. By this method, each print is unique.

When exact control over where color will appear in a series of prints is desired, more rigid technical procedures should be used. These require the use of more than one block. The illustrations in this chapter show some possible ways of creating color prints with more than one block.

The Kiss by Edvard Munch, 1902. (Collection The Museum of Modern Art, New York. Gift of Abby Aldrich Rockefeller.)

This famous print is one of the finest examples of the use of natural wood texture as an important part of the design. Imagine the print without it! The figures, cut in one block, were printed first, in black. The second block, the wood texture, was printed over the figures, in gray. Printing light over dark is unusual because in most prints the dark shows through the light, which can be undesirable. Here, however, it obviously works.

Two Horses by Ewald Mataré, 1950.
(Collection The Museum of Modern Art,
New York.)

The grain in this block is unusually
distinct. It is possible to enhance the grain
of wood by soaking the block in water to
soften it and then rubbing along the grain
with a stiff bristle brush or steel wool.

Opposite page
Voyage to the Bottom of the Sea
by Joel Erickson.

Two separate images can be combined to
enhance each other. Here the sun
gives dramatic focus to the silhouette of
the submarine, a subject inspired by
the seven-year-old artist's favorite
television program. Two separate pieces
of linoleum were roughly cut with
scissors into the basic shapes. The sun
was carved and printed first. The block
bearing the sun was moved over the print
until the artist found "just the right
spot" to print it.

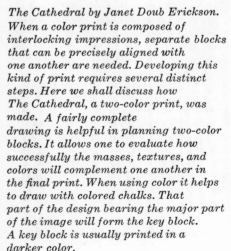

1. The key block.

2.

The Cathedral by Janet Doub Erickson. When a color print is composed of interlocking impressions, separate blocks that can be precisely aligned with one another are needed. Developing this kind of print requires several distinct steps. Here we shall discuss how The Cathedral, a two-color print, was made. A fairly complete drawing is helpful in planning two-color blocks. It allows one to evaluate how successfully the masses, textures, and colors will complement one another in the final print. When using color it helps to draw with colored chalks. That part of the design bearing the major part of the image will form the key block. A key block is usually printed in a darker color.

When the drawing pleases you, cut two sheets of backing board, larger than the drawing. The backings should be exactly the same size. Because this print is large, the backings are of Masonite. Heavy cardboard is adequate for smaller prints.

Cut a sheet of linoleum slightly larger than the image in the drawing; this will be the key block. Glue the linoleum on one of the backing boards, and begin cutting the design. When the image is well worked out, stop, leave it unfinished until you can see how it—and its companion block—interact.

2. Proof of the key block. Prepare a printing bed (See "Technical Notes") and lay a proof sheet over it. Here you may have to work quickly. Ink the key block heavily and press it down on the proof sheet. Before you take the block off, mark its corners on the proof sheet. Then lift the block off and lay it aside.

3. Second backing board with offset print. Pick up the second backing board, line it up with the corner marks, and set it down on the proof sheet. Press it so that the ink transfers to the board, and then pick up the board. The image on the key block has now been offset onto the second backing board.

3.

4.

5.

4. Second backing board with linoleum glued over offset print. *The shapes of those areas that are to provide a second color should now be cut out of linoleum and glued into place. (You could have offset the key block onto an entire sheet of linoleum, however, is a cheaper and easier method. It saves time in cutting away unwanted areas and saves linoleum.)*

In gluing pieces of linoleum over the offset print, you have, of course, obscured the details to be matched and cut. To define them again, you will have to make a second offset print of your first block. The procedure is the same. Put a lot of ink on the key block, press it down onto a fresh proof sheet, mark off the corners, and *position the second color block—this time with the linoleum glued in place—on the marks. The image transferred onto the second color block will give you the guide lines for cutting.*

5. Second block cut and ready for two-color proof. *When the second block has been worked, you are ready to make a two-color proof. You will usually want to print the lighter color first because it generally forms part of the background. Ink the color onto the block and press it onto the proof sheet; again mark the corners. Then ink the second block, align it with the guide marks, and set it down. It is not necessary to wait for the first color to dry; it probably will have already been absorbed into the paper.* *Now you have a two-color proof for study. If you are satisfied, finish any uncut areas and make a final print. If greater detail or more elements seem necessary, work them out. For example, the first print made from these blocks was gray and black. The scene was somber, cold, and lifeless—like a massive stone edifice early on a dank, cold morning. The print was complete. Another print made from the same blocks was printed in yellow and black. It suggested late afternoon on a brisk, sunny day. The print seemed incomplete, but adding pigeons exploding into flight in front of the cathedral finished it.*

The Violinist by Eugene Larkin, 1957.
(Courtesy The Print Council Of America,
New York City.)

In this two-color woodcut the major part
of the image was conceived on one block
and printed in black. The lighter block
formed a background of roughly
descriptive shadows over which the key
block was printed.

Fighting Cock by Walter Williams, 1957. (Courtesy The Print Council of America, New York City.)

The black key block is very realistic and definitive and the forms are clearly recognizable. The freely cut orange background block adds emotional tension—even a small amount of concentrated color is important.

From a Brecht Poem: Auschwitz by Antonio Frasconi. (Courtesy The Print Council of America, New York City.)

At first glance one sees only the mass. The second color block gives an overall tonality that prevents one from picking out the details—each painful. The mass is a solid monument to horror.

Work Kanae by Haku Maki. (Collection The Museum of Modern Art, New York.)

Bold black swaths are dramatically set off by the intricate, introspective pattern of the lighter colored block.

Collision by Robert Conover, 1958. (Courtesy The Print Council of America, New York City.)

The splintered fragments breaking away from the massive, almost architectural, collision of forms were cut with a knife. The gouge just doesn't make that kind of line. The lighter forms provide an echo of the collision.

Evening (Melancholy) (On the Beach) by Edvard Munch, 1896. (Collection The Museum of Modern Art, New York. Abby Aldrich Rockefeller Fund.)

There are four separate blocks here: three to give color areas and one to give an all-over wood texture. The quality of the wood grain is subtly used to unify flat color areas. Notice on the bottom edge how the blocks overlapped.

*Horses Resting (Ruhende Pferde) by Franz Mark, 1911. (Collection The Museum of
Modern Art, New York. Gift of Abby Aldrich Rockefeller.)*

*Color, as used by Franz Marc and other Expressionists, cuts across the shapes to create a
pattern independent of naturalistically conceived forms. Thus this print has two visual
images: the abstract and the naturalistic.*

Seated Woman, After Cranach by Pablo
Picasso, 1958. (Collection The Museum of
Modern Art, New York. Gift of Mr. and
Mrs. Daniel Saidenberg.)

Three separate linoleum blocks were
registered to make this portrait. Its
liveliness derives directly from the way
the broad gouge has been used to create
the background.

Portable Shrine by Yoshitoshi Mori, 1958.
(Collection The Museum of Modern Art,
New York.)

The principle of using two wood blocks for
color woodcuts is the same as that of using
two linoleum blocks. Here the design is
enhanced by the strong texture of the rice
paper on which it is printed.

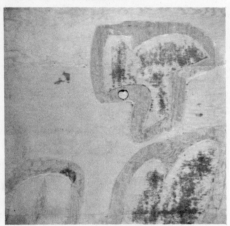

Tree by Carol Summers (Courtesy of the artist.) See Frontispiece.

As you gain experience in making prints with more than one block, new ideas will occur to you. Here we have one technique developed by Carol Summers, a famous American print maker. Mr. Summers frequently works in plywood, and he uses both sides of the block. He can do this because of the way in which he prints his blocks.

The four sheets of plywood are the same size. As you can see in the photographs, the shapes are roughly outlined by cutting narrow bands around them. Mr. Summers lays the paper, usually a soft, textured Japanese paper which is quite thin, over the block and inks the paper over the outlined shapes with a brayer. His technique resembles making a rubbing, but he uses ink instead of chalk. Notice that these blocks, although used several times, are quite clean. They have never been directly inked.

When the first impression, or rubbing, has been made, the artist lays the paper over the other blocks. Because he is working with the relief face up and because the paper is slightly transparent, he can position his paper more or less by eye.

In the final print you can see that the edges are soft rather than hard, as is typical of most woodcuts. This is due to the rubbing technique. In other prints in which he desires an even softer edge, Mr. Summers wets the paper around the relief with an ink thinner. Then as he lays the ink on it runs. How much it runs depends on how wet the paper is.

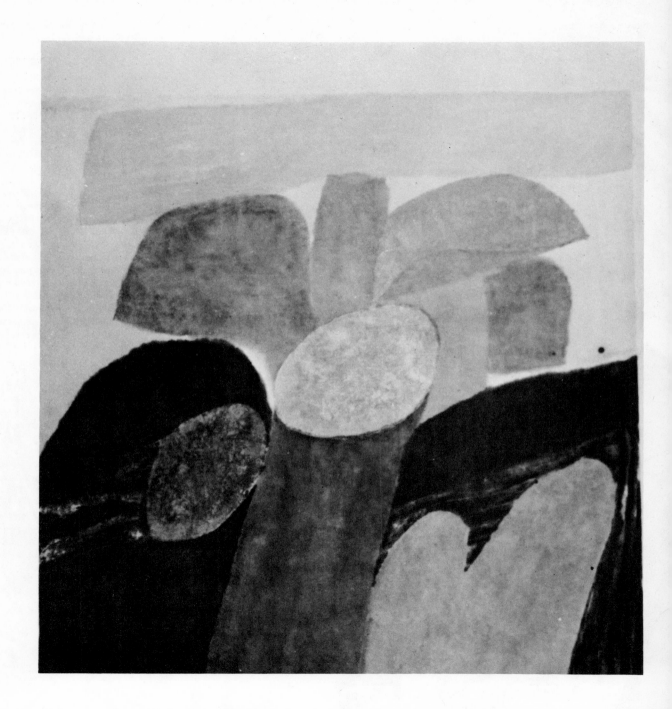

Vis-A-Vis by Seong Moy, 1962. (Courtesy The Print Council of America, New York City.)

Here wood relief is used in an entirely different way: to create small flat color areas to build up the form.

Jonah On the Ship by Sadeo Watanabe, 1959. (Collection The Museum of Modern Art, New York.)

Color may be used as an integral part of the design or as a decorative element. In this print the color blocks were used as a luxurious addition. The whole design is carried by the key block, which by itself forms a complete statement.

Opposite page
Winter Moonlight by Ernst L. Kirchner, 1918. (Collection The Museum of Modern Art, New York.)

Here three color blocks create the effect of a fourth color. The semitransparent color of the trees together with the underlying darker color give the effect of a third color.

Kabuki Players as the Eight Sennin (Triptych) by Kininaga (Utagawa), died ca. 1820. (Courtesy The Cooper Union Museum, New York City).

Japanese woodcuts had an important influence on Western art. The stylized poses and decoratively abstracted drapery and natural forms led into Art Nouveau. The elimination of nonessentials and the flat treatment of color areas as well as the use of line influenced the Post Impressionists.

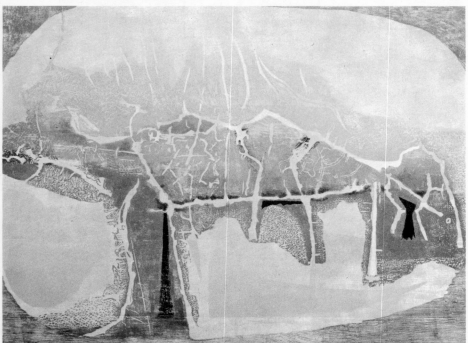

Continental Divide by Worden Day. (Courtesy The Brooklyn Museum.)

Deliberately carved fine texture effectively contrasts with the natural grain of the wood. An almost painterly use of separate colors can be seen in the mountain-like shapes in the midground of the print.

*Performers of Sacred Music by Yoshitoshi
Mori, 1959. (Collection The Museum of
Modern Art, New York.)*

*Try to imagine this print as consisting of
only the dark block. Here color is used to
organize otherwise indistinguishable
forms. Without the unifying areas of
color, the print would be unfinished.*

Left: *Dallas 1963 by Antonio Frasconi,
1964. (Courtesy The Brooklyn Museum.)*

*Mass and bold form contrast for emotional
effect. Wood texture binds the
anonymous figures into the composition
and sets them up as a foil for one of
the most horrifying and tragic events in
recent American history.*

Opposite page
Top: *The Fulton Fish Market by
Antonio Frasconi, 1952. (Collection
The Museum of Modern Art, New York.
Inter-American Fund.)*

*Look closely at each of the prints in this
series. Two seperate blocks, the
buildings and their signs, are repeated in
each to create the same locale. But
each scene has been made with different
overprinted blocks. The group of
four separate prints depicts the
24-hour-a-day panorama of Fulton Street.*

Bottom: *Florentine Sunset by Carl Rantz.*

*In this description of architecture in a
famous old city, the influence of the
cutting tools is obvious. The openings in
the buildings are simple, single-cut
gouge marks in wood. It appears that three
impressions have been made: a dark
one for the buildings, a medium one for
distant cityscape and the sun, and a
light one for the sky and pavement.*

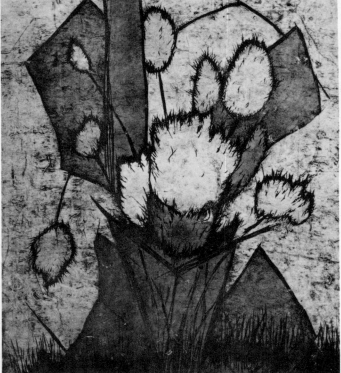

Opposite page
Top: *City Night by Janet Doub Erickson.*

In this eight-color linoleum print color has been used to describe the image, not to decorate it. The scene represents the patterns of artificial light seen in the city after dark.

Bottom: *Floral Arrangement by Margaret Philbrick.*

This design of abstract flowers was printed from two Masonite blocks. Masonite is a thin, lightweight, rigid building panel made of pressed wood fibers. One side is very smooth, the other quite rough. Both can be used in print making. Medium hard in density, Masonite can be readily cut with wood or linoleum gouges. When cut with some tools, however, it shreds and crumbles to dust, which may be irritating to the lungs. If this becomes a problem, a gauze mask can be used.

Right: *The Dog and the Crocodile by Antonio Frasconi, 1950. (Courtesy The Brooklyn Museum.)*

Woodcuts can amuse and tell a tale. The character of both beasts is captured here, and from their juxtaposition you can almost make up the story. Notice how finely gouged lines have been used on the back of the crocodile.

Bandbox, American, about 1830. (Courtesy The Cooper Union Museum, New York.)

Block printing may be used to enhance common objects. Wallpapers and fabrics were printed from wood blocks before the advent of photo-mechanical processes. Some of the designs, when isolated from their practical applications, stand up as works of art.

The bandbox depicted here has been covered with wallpaper. The design has bounce and life. It is charmingly naive, and the hatbox must have been a treasured possession.

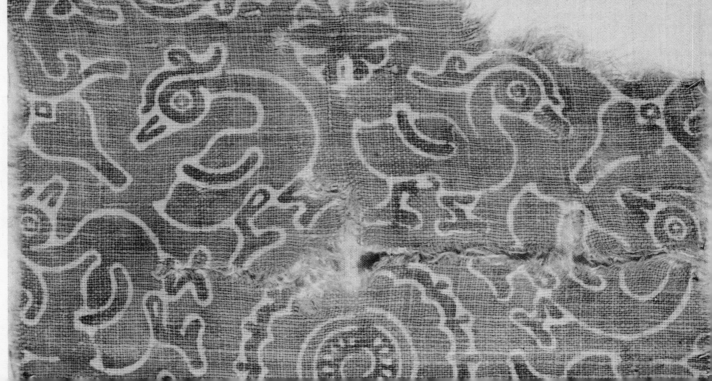

Black Bar by Michael Rothenstein.
(Courtesy The Brooklyn Museum.)

*The varied wood textures complement one
another. The delicacy and direction of
the grains are dramatically contrasted
with the black forms, which are
completely unrelated to typical woodcut
forms.*

Opposite page
Top: *Manao Tu Papau (The Spirits of the
Dead Watching)* by Paul Gauguin.
*(Collection Museum of Fine Arts, Boston.
Gift of W. G. Russell Allen.)*

*Gauguin's woodcuts are boldly designed
and carried out without loosing the spirit
of the wood plank. In the landscape,
sensitive indications of texture and
direction have been achieved by leaving
traces of the gouge.*

*This is an artist's proof, not a finished
print. Some part of the print making
process needs improvement: note on the
dog at left that the two impressions
are not aligned.*

Bottom: *Plain Cloth Printed with Ducks
and Rosettes, North India (1250-1370).
Found in Fostat, Egypt. (Courtesy The
Cooper Union Museum, New York.)*

*This ancient textile was printed from two
registered wood blocks in dull red
and brown. It is difficult to distinguish how
the reliefs were composed, so cleverly
was it done. It appears that, using the
large rosette as the center of a circle and
the ducks as the periphery, half the
circle was cut in two sets of blocks. Note
how the central rosette is slightly
off register.*

Palazzo Malatesta, Rimini by Carol Summers, 1962. (Courtesy The Print Council of America, New York City.)

Here the elements suggest, rather than define, architecture and other forms. They are reduced to symbols rather than specifics. Broad colored areas have been overprinted with simple forms.

*Mandala by Vincent Longo. (Courtesy
The Print Council of America,
New York City.)*

*In this color woodcut a three-dimensional
effect has been created by printing
rich, opaque color over other impressions
whose edges provide cast shadows for
the overprint.*

The Hunt by Howard Cross, age 11. (Courtesy of Burnett Cross.)

One of the easiest to cut and cheapest materials for making a stamp print is the common potato. Here one half of the potato was used for the hunters and the other half for the hunted. The scene was printed with poster paint in three colors—brown, orange, and blue—on construction paper. The lighter impressions were made by using the potato without re-inking it. Notice that the fight was not entirely one-sided, the animals got one hunter.

Opposite page

Turtles by Jane Craig, Cambridge, Mass.

This artist is known as "The Potato Printer" because she uses this vegetable often and in a most versatile manner. Here she has overprinted impressions made with quarters of potato with other impressions, also cut from a potato. Working with potatoes has one disadvantage if you wish to make numerous prints over a period of days. Potatoes dry out, distorting the design.

Stamp Prints, Monoprints and Mixed Media

STAMP PRINTS

Anything that is durable enough to be
incised or cut into a relief can be used as a
stamp to make a print. Potatoes, paraffin
blocks, clay, and other common materials
will serve. Also, anything that can be cut
and pasted on a flat surface can be used
as a stamp. Here are only a few examples;
you can probably think of other ways to
make stamp prints.

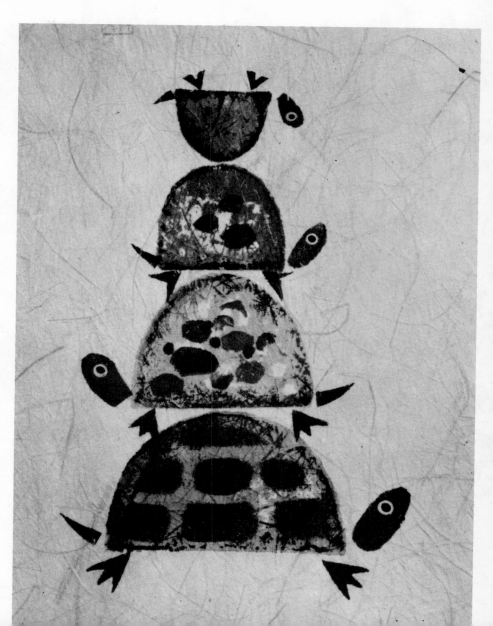

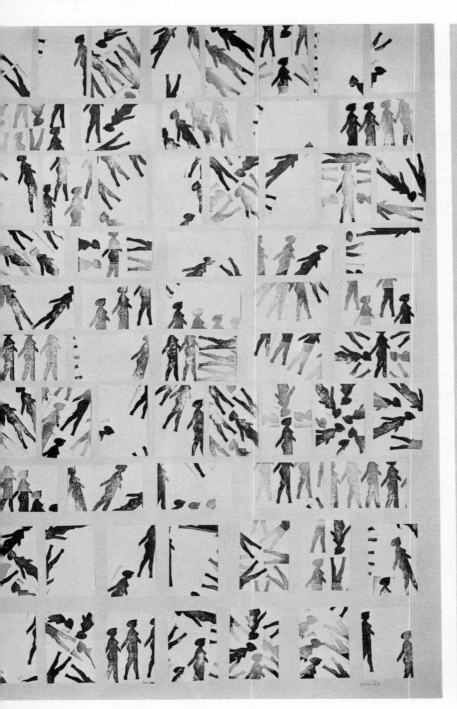

Garden by a student at the Craft Workshop at the YWCA, Boston.

Scissors and a very sharp gouge were used to cut a flower motif from an old rubber inner tube. The cutout was then glued on a cardboard backing board, and inked with a pounce. The motif was printed twice, in two colors, on a light-weight cotton fabric.

Opposite page
Left: *Shot!* by Michael Snow, 1963. (Collection The Museum of Modern Art, New York.)

The artist made a single, small rubber cutout figure of a woman and stamped it at random on 63 different sheets of paper. Then he arranged the printed sheets in rows on a large piece of paper, and glued them down. The resulting montage makes an exciting print.

Ten Little Indians by Janet Doub Erickson.

A wide, deep gouge was used to cut one little Indian in a 3 by 5-inch block of household paraffin. The block was rolled with deep blue ink and printed (by standing on it!) on a length of orange linen. The ends of the fabric were hemmed and sticks inserted in the hems to keep the material from curling. The whole thing was hung, banner-like, in a small boy's room.

Clay Prints by preschool children.

These charming impressions were made by preschool children in the same manner as the previous clay prints. The children used red clay blocks they made themselves with clay they dug from a riverbank.

Mother and Child by Albert Jacobson.

The almost sculptural look of this small print suggests the solid quality of the clay slab from which the impression was made.

Elephant Dance by a student in the art division of the State University of New York College for Teachers at Buffalo, New York.

Linoleum gouges were used to cut an elephant in a large Artgum eraser. The first elephant was printed on another Artgum eraser, which was then cut out in a similar manner. The two mirror images were printed as a fanciful interpretation of elephant behavior.

Sandpipers by Jane Craig, Cambridge, Mass.

Several techniques, including stamp printing with potatoes, were used to make this sprightly print. Color was rolled across the top with a brayer to make the horizon and rolled over a cardboard cutout laid over the bottom to make the wavy edge of the sea. Between these two areas dart the sea birds, whose bodies were printed with potatoes, the legs with the side of a piece of cardboard dipped in ink. The birds' eyes were touched in with the end of a pencil.

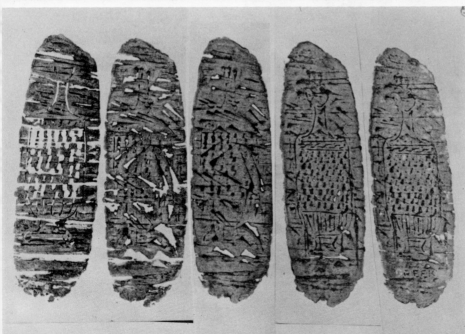

Greek by Albert Jacobson.

This series was made from the same stamp—a block of moist, gray potter's clay rolled flat and incised with a pointed modeling stick. No ink was needed, because moist clay adheres to paper and leaves a thin layer as the print. No two prints made from a clay stamp are exactly alike. It is extremely difficult to keep a consistent amount of moisture on the surface of the clay, and the impression becomes distorted as you pull the clay off the paper.

All-Over Pattern by an elementary
education student at the State University
of New York College for Teachers at
Buffalo, New York.

A sharp knife was used to cut a simple
design in the end of a rubber eraser.
Stamped on black paper in red poster
paint, it became a colorful and
unusual gift wrapping.

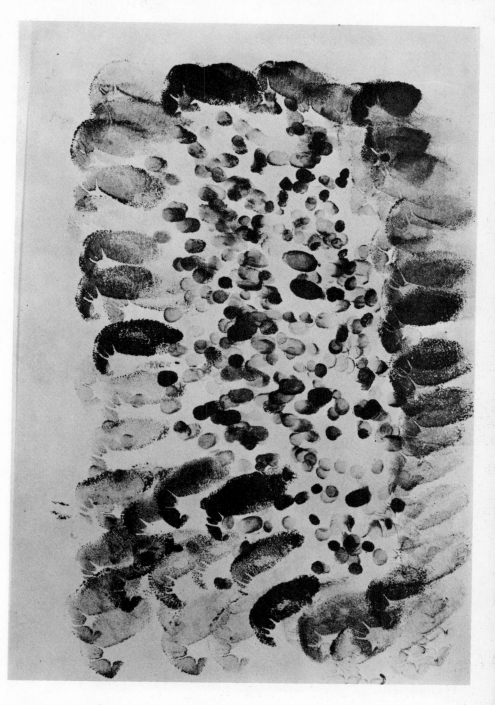

The simplest way to print is a monoprint. Here a fourth grader put his fingers and palm into a thin coat of ink and printed. The result is interesting and can be called a monoprint because it was made by a printing method that permits the making of only one print. The print was made while the child was listening to music with a strong beat.

MONOPRINTS AND TRANSFER DRAWINGS

The term monoprint, or monotype, refers to those prints that have been made by a printing process that permits the taking of only one impression. The most familiar method is the following: Oils, watercolors, or printer's inks are used to paint a picture on a hard, nonabsorbent surface like glass or a metal plate. While the color is still wet—and it may be for some time, since the surface absorbs none of the color—a sheet of paper is laid over it. The paper is then rubbed with a brayer or the hand, or sometimes even run through a press, to make the color transfer. Since most of the color transfers in one printing, only one print can be made—a monoprint.

Another printing method that permits the production of only one print is commonly called transfer drawing, to distinguish it from the method described above. In transfer drawing, a palette or some other nonabsorbent surface is spread with a thin coat of thick printer's ink. A sheet of paper is laid over the ink surface, and the artist draws on the paper. Drawing on the paper causes ink to transfer to those areas pressed by the drawing tool. When the sheet of paper is peeled off the plate, the print on the back of the drawing is the mirror image of the drawing. Naturally this transfer drawing technique permits the making of only one print.

Woman With Parasol by Maurice
Prendergast, 1901. (Collection The
Museum of Modern Art, New York.
Gift of Mr. and Mrs. Arthur B. Altschul.)

A famous American Impressionist
brushed paint onto a metal plate, making
the delicately hued sketch from which
the monoprint impression of a
turn-of-the-century lady was taken.

Ave Maria by Paul Gauguin.
(Courtesy Museum of Fine Arts, Boston.)

Paint was brushed onto a plate and an impression taken. After printing the impression, Gauguin added light watercolor washes for more interest.

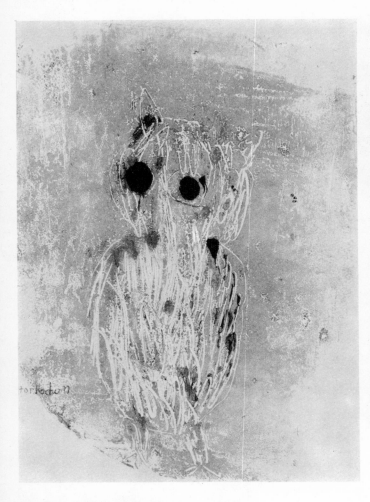

House by Joel Erickson.

Owl by a student at the Shady Hill School, Cambridge, Mass.

To make this monoprint, water-base printer's ink was rolled out on a sheet of glass and the lines drawn with a pointed stick. The thick blobs of blue ink dropped on the face as eyes flattened out under pressure, achieving an entirely owlish expression.

This spontaneous monoprint is a transfer drawing. A pointed stick was used as a drawing tool on the back of a sheet of paper laid gently on an inked palette. The impression is formed by ink picked up on the face of the paper.

Sometimes when making transfer drawings there is too much ink on the palette, and the paper sinks into it as you lay it down. If this happens, lay one or two sheets of newsprint over the palette until the excess ink is blotted up. You can tell that the palette is ready when the paper lies lightly over the ink and doesn't immediately begin absorbing ink without your pressing on it.

Top
Cheshire Cat by a student at the
Shady Hill School, Cambridge, Mass.

Lines were drawn into black oil paint
spread on a sheet of metal. Paper laid on
top of the wet image was rolled with a
brayer and rubbed with the back of a
spoon to pick up the impression.

Bottom
Wax Resist Monoprint by a
student at the Massachusetts College of
Art, Boston.

The textured background in this
experimental monoprint was made by
rubbing a sheet of aluminum with
a wax crayon. The whole area was then
washed over with watercolor, and
the dark areas added with black drawing
ink. Paper laid down over the metal
sheet and rolled with a wide, soft brayer
picked up this evocative impression.

Roman Arch I by Carol Summers.

*Here both the drawing and the printed
impression are shown. You can clearly
see that one is the mirror image of
the other.*

Roman Arch II by Carol Summers.

*In this variation of the arch theme,
notice how the ink has picked up around
the line as well as on the line itself.
The area where more concentrated
drawing was done picked up more ink.*

STENCILED PRINTS

A stencil is a flat sheet with perforations in it. The perforations may form a word or a design. Stencil paper can be bought in art supply stores, or you can make your own. Any kind of flat material can be used to make a stencil. Thin cardboard, the kind used as shirtboards or to back pads of paper, is quite adequate. If you are improvising your own stencil from cardboard or paper, you must make it nonabsorbent to prevent it from absorbing the inks or paints. A stencil that absorbs colors can lead to smeared images, which are usually quite undesirable. To make your stencil nonabsorbent, heat paraffin in a flat pan until it melts and dip your stencil in it. Be careful, because the paraffin will be quite hot. The resulting waxed stencil has an added advantage: you can easily wipe ink or print from it when you wish to change color.

The larger the image to be cut out, the sturdier the stencil material should be. Since you are cutting out part of it, the sheet can become loose and floppy and hard to handle. However, no matter what material you choose, it should be thin enough to allow the brayer to reach the paper easily. By a little experimentation, you will quickly find the material suitable to your purposes.

Stencil Printing.

Here a simple motif cut from a stencil is being used. Notice that the stencil is sturdy enough to be handled easily, yet thin enough for a brush, or brayer, to come into contact with the paper. Printer's ink or any other non-runny material is adequate for stenciling. The stenciled print, unlike the design printed from a relief motif, faces in the same direction as the stencil.

The Building Walks at Night by Yasuo
Kobashi, 1958. (Collection The Museum
of Modern Art, New York.)

A sheet of cardboard with perforated
designs was inked in different colors with
broad strokes of the brayer, and then
printed on dark paper. The result is a
rather spooky impression.

PAPER RELIEF PRINTS

Anything can be used to make a relief, including paper. Shapes may be cut out of cardboard, tag board, illustration board or any other kind of paper and glued onto heavy cardboard or Masonite. The resulting relief block may be printed face up, like a wood block, or face down, like a linoleum block.

Plant Life by Jim Forsberg. (Courtesy The Print Council of America, New York City.)

Bold shapes of a heavily textured cardboard were cut out, mounted, and printed like a woodcut to make this strongly patterned cardboard print.

Top
Elephant by a fifth grade student at Shady Hill School, Cambridge, Mass.

This gay pink pachyderm was outlined with a sharp knife on a piece of corrugated cardboard. Then the top layer of paper was peeled off the cardboard around the elephant to reveal a circus stripe background. The relief was printed face up on a thin sheet of paper.

Bottom
Cocks by Charles Smith, 1939. (Collection The Museum of Modern Art, New York.)

A single rooster cutout was inked and printed in four different positions for the bodies. Eyes, tail feathers, and feet were added with other cutouts. Motion has been suggested by moving the cutouts during printing. The blurred legs may have been made by dragging the inked edge of a piece of cardboard across the paper.

Rock Cross by Edmund Casarella.
(Courtesy The Brooklyn Museum.)

This complex, carefully built up
multicolor print was made from a series of
paper reliefs. Overprinting, and therefore
registered blocks, is obviously involved.

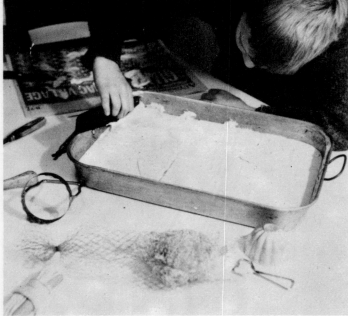

Race Week by several Ericksons, a family effort.

This figure briefly summarizes how to make a plaster print and what goes wrong with it. Joel, pictured here, is making a seascape in an oblong block of plaster of paris. While it is still wet, he is scratching and incising it with various tools, including a large comb. When the block was dry, it was removed from the pan. This took three children: Evie to support the plaster, as the pan was being held upside down; Andrew to pat the back of the pan to dislodge the block, and Sally to carefully loosen the edges with a knife.

The block was removed intact, and was then carefully and gently inked with a brayer. Many of the more delicate furrows broke, and the brayer and palette became clogged with bits of plaster— a nasty mess. But we still didn't give up. Thin tissue paper was laid over the inked block and rubbed very gently with a clean, soft pounce. A few nice textures were picked up from the sea and sky, and then the plaster rewarded our efforts by breaking. Since we had a partial print and had spent so much time on it, we finished it by stenciling sails on it with a brayer. Considering the time and effort, we recommend that you channel your artistic efforts into a more rewarding form of print making.

PLASTER PRINTS

Plaster print is a rather misleading term. It suggests that a design is made in plaster and a print made from that design. Many people have tried this, but it really doesn't work too well. However, here is the general process for those who wish to try. Plaster of paris and/or spackle— a calking compound—are mixed and poured into a shallow greased pan or cardboard box. Just before the plaster sets, various tools can be used on it. The resulting image is usually composed of shallow impressions bordered by furrows of displaced plaster. When the plaster dries, it is ready for printing. At this point usually one of two things happens: Either the plaster block breaks as you are removing it from the pan or, if you had the foresight to cast the block in a cardboard box so that you could peel the sides away from the block, the plaster cracks while you are inking or printing it.

Cycle of a Large Sea: Unbeing Myself by Arthur Deshaies, 1961. (Courtesy The Brooklyn Museum.)

This is a plaster relief print, which is actually a kind of plaster cast. To make a plaster relief print, a relief is made by engraving a metal plate or carving a wood block. Then the face of the plate or block is framed with a snug-fitting, shadow-box-like wood frame. The plate is inked, the frame replaced, and a thin layer of plaster of paris poured into the frame over the inked plate. Before it dries, the plaster block is reinforced with tongue depressors or metal rods. When dry, the plaster block separates readily from the oily, inked plate. Typical of this technique are the brilliant black and white contrasts seen in this figure.

*Flocked Wall Hanging, Sweden, 15th
century. (Courtesy The Cooper Union
Museum, New York.)*

*Here a wood block was spread with
glue and printed. Into the glue was
sprinkled flock, pulverized bits of wool or
cotton fibers. Today flock can be
obtained from wallpaper manufacturers,
or made by grinding cotton felt with
a mortar and pestle.*

MIXED MEDIA

This section includes some interesting uses of the basic print making techniques. Some of the examples are only fragments of former masterworks, but they contain the germs of ideas that may be used for experimentation.

Top
Illustration by Joan Miro for
A Toute Epreuve, *a book by Paul Eluard, published in 1958. (Collection The Museum of Modern Art, New York. Gift of Mr. and Mrs. Walter Bareiss.)*

Print making can be combined with any other art technique. This color woodcut was combined with collage; the string was glued over the woodcut.

Bottom
Silk Fragment from a Lady's Kimono, Japan, late 17th—early 18th century. (Courtesy The Cooper Union Museum, New York.)

Here stenciling was combined with tie-dying. The clarity of the lines in the dark curly-cue design and in the flowers indicates that they were stenciled. The large light areas were tie-dyed. Each little square represents a separate tying process. A tiny bit of material was forced into a peak and the peak tied. When all the peaks had been tied, the stenciled areas were coated with wax and the fabric dabbed with dye. Excruciatingly painstaking hand labor like this is now faked by machine processes, but at one time it must have been a labor of love and a great satisfaction to the craftsman.

Fragment from a Lady's Kimono, Japan, late 17th—early 18th century. (Courtesy The Cooper Union Museum, New York.)

Embroidery, printing with relief blocks, and stenciling were frequently combined in the Orient to make richly designed fabrics. In this beautiful fragment stenciling was used in the dark areas to relieve the tedium of a large mass. The pattern is light and hard to distinguish in the photograph, but it successfully serves its purpose on the fabric. The star-like flowers were also stenciled. Two types of embroidery are represented, the straight stitch and couching. In couching, as seen in the waves made of gold threads, the thread was laid on top of the material and tacked down with tiny, almost invisible stitches.

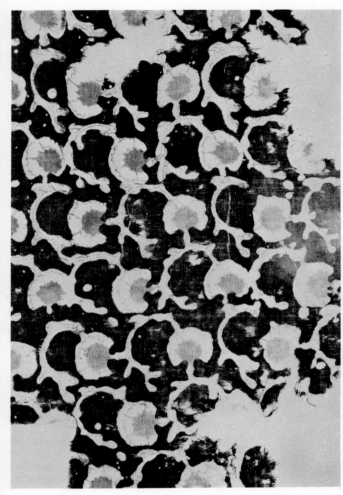

Printed Linen, Germany, 12th to 13th
century. (Courtesy The Cooper Union
Museum, New York.)

The exquisite design on this textile
was printed from wood relief blocks in an
unusual manner: Glue was rolled over
the block and printed on dark blue linen.
While the print was still wet, an alloy
of copper, tin, and zinc ground into dust
was sprinkled on it. You see the result.
The fabric was probably used for
decorative purposes, as the wear and tear
of everyday use would have cracked
the glue or worn off the alloy.

Textile fragment, India, 14th-16th century
(found in Fostat, Egypt). (Courtesy
The Cooper Union Museum, New York.)

In this textile fragment, an overall
floral pattern was block printed in first.
Then the fabric was batiked twice.
In batik, wax is brushed over areas of the
fabric, making them impermeable.
Then the fabric is dipped in dye. Only the
unprotected areas take the dye.
After the fabric dries, the wax is removed
by pressing with a warm iron.

6

Technical Notes

The equipment for print making without a press is simple, and the supplies inexpensive. A half dozen things make up a basic kit. Additional materials, such as cardboard, linoleum, carrots and plaster, are easily available. The tools or knives useful in working designs into the various surfaces are simple and not difficult to learn to use. A basic print-making kit should consist of the following:

1. A smooth, hard palette on which to mix and spread inks. A 9″ x 12″ piece of glass, marble, or metal is best, but Masonite, celluloid, or shellacked cardboard will serve.

2. A roller or brayer for spreading ink evenly. The most satisfactory kind of brayer is a gelatine or soft rubber roller mounted in a metal handle. Brayers with hard rubber rollers should be avoided; they are harder to use successfully. The roller should be about six inches long and an inch or more in diameter. There are smaller and larger brayers available, but

the six-inch size is more than adequate for most projects. For small size prints, a fabric pounce will work well. A pounce can be made easily by stuffing a rag into the toe of an old sock. The stuffed toe should be tied to form a ball.

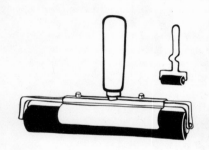

3. Several spatulas or stiff oil painting knives to use in handling the inks on the palette.

4. Inks. A printing ink of fairly thick consistency is best for most printing projects.

Oil-base printer's inks may be obtained from printers' suppliers. These inks come in several different qualities, and are made by many different companies. Sold by weight in small or large tins or tubes, inks vary in price according to the quality of the color. Simple earth colors are cheaper than the more chemically complex tones.

The firms that make printing inks also manufacture "transparent base" and extender. Transparent base is a jelly-like substance which enables you to print a transparent film of color. Mix a small amount of color with the base and experiment until you achieve the proper transparency. Extender, or "base white," is mixed with color to make it go further. Extender does not change the tinting power of the original color but it will lighten it noticeably if used in quantity. Opaque white, or "cover white," should be used on fabric or to lighten colors which must be opaque. Since the manufacturers' names for these substances vary greatly, it is wise to experiment with the brands available to you.

Water-base printer's ink, which is sold by most art and craft supply shops, has much the same consistency as the oil-base ink. Being soluble in water, it is easily rinsed from tools and other equipment, and hands and clothes can be cleaned with soap and water. Of course it should not be used on paper that is printed damp or used to print fabrics. Also water-base inks should never be used to print fabrics because they wash out easily and will run during printing, as fabrics are printed damp.

Poster paints or watercolors can be used when making prints from vegetables, or for special transparent effects when working with wood blocks.

5. Solvents for thinning and cleaning up. Boiled linseed oil is used to thin oil-base inks if they become too stiff to handle. However, use caution—too much linseed oil will cause the ink to bleed and spread, making a blurred print.

6. Paint rags are indispensable for keeping hands and tools clean and usable. Newspapers may be used to protect the work table. Always keep a stack of old newspapers handy.

7. Printing bed. When printing a block face down, a printing bed is needed. An adequate printing bed can be made on a smooth section of floor or on a table top. Lay out a good thick pad of newspapers, unfolding each paper and smoothing the sheets out individually. Overlap the edges so that you can feel no lumps when you run your fingers firmly over the pad. A pad about one-eighth inch thick is usually soft enough.

Not essential, but helpful, is a sheet of the soft fiber wallboard called "Homosote" to use as a printing bed. Sold by lumber dealers it comes in 4 x 6-foot, and 4 x 8-foot panels. It is inexpensive. You can cut Homosote to the size you need with a sharp knife or saw. A thin pad of newspapers over it will make a sufficiently soft bed. A wooden or Masonite drawing board can be used instead of the Homosote, but it must be padded with a thicker layer of newspapers.

BRIEF GUIDE TO PAPERS AND FABRICS
FOR PRINT MAKING

What you print on will very much affect the way the print looks.

Soft absorbent surfaces are easiest to print. In general it is best to avoid paper with a smooth, hard, shiny finish. This kind of surface will repel paint as well as printing ink. Also under the pressure of printing, the inked block may skid, making a blurred print.

For many experiments newsprint is adequate.

Most colored "construction paper" has a fairly hard, smooth surface that is tricky to print on cleanly, although it can be done with care. The strong, bright colors are interesting to work with; the darker tones and black are particularly effective printed with white.

Inexpensive, medium weight rice paper takes a print beautifully. Made in Japan, it is available in many different textures

and colors from art supply stores and some stationery shops. You will also find it rewarding to experiment with some of the unusual and very beautiful rice papers sold by those companies dealing in fine papers for graphic designers and printers. Japanese importing companies sometimes stock rice papers, as well as ink and brushes.

Domestic printing papers similar to rice paper are now available. Made from cotton, rayon, and sometimes other fibers, they are very satisfactory. They often can be purchased in rolls from school supply companies, as well as in sheets from art supply stores.

Fabric, naturally soft and absorbent, is wonderful to print on, and hand printed fabrics can be used for all kinds of decorative purposes.

Fabric printed with good quality, oil-base printer's ink is completely washable when dry. Drape printed lengths carefully over a rack or clothes line and allow them to dry for three to five days.

Today an infinite variety of beautiful textiles from all over the world is available. Colors, weaves, and textures are combined in endless ways. Muslin and pieces of old sheeting are fine for some prints, but try felt, velveteen, satin, burlap, and suede cloth, as well as the more common cottons and linens. Experimenting with different colors and values on these varying textures may open up unsuspected possibilities to further develop a design.

Fabric shops frequently sell short, leftover pieces of materials at bargain prices. This is an inexpensive source of the more beautiful and unusual fabrics for experimental purposes.

Synthetic fabrics, including Fiberglas, usually take a print very well. Try a test print to be sure. Heavy woolens should be used carefully. The wool fiber absorbs the printing ink easily enough, but then it keeps on absorbing it. Sometimes after several months the print will become noticeably faint, and may finally disappear completely.

Most linen, cotton, and synthetic

fabrics have a starch solution added during the final part of the manufacturing process. This starch is soluble in water, and should be rinsed away before fabric is printed, otherwise the first time the piece is washed after printing, the starch will dissolve and take some of the print with it. Long lengths of heavy fabric can be put through a washing machine; shorter lengths and more delicate textures need only be soaked a few minutes in a bucket of lukewarm water just before printing. Since many fabrics take a print best when damp, wetting the fabric thoroughly before printing serves these two purposes. The newspapers that make up the printing bed also form a blotting pad that soaks up excess water, then stays damp so that the fabric does not dry out while you are working on it.

Felt, velveteen, satin, and other fabrics that are not usually washed can be printed dry, as can burlap and Fiberglas. Fine, light silks also seem to print as well dry as wet.

It is very important to adjust the consistency of your ink to the weight and texture of the paper or fabric that you are printing on. A thick, soft rice paper, heavy drapery fabric or felt will take a good strong image from a thickly inked block. However, to make a clean print on fine, thin paper or on a light weight silk or cotton, use a much more thinly inked block.

PRINTING ON FABRIC

Before being printed, long lengths of fabric should be cut to the size they will be when used. This not only makes bulky yardage easy to handle, but also allows you to plan and print the design so that it fits nicely into the finished length. Be sure to leave enough material at both the top and bottom of each length to turn under for hems and headings. An additional allowance should be made for any shrinkage that may take place in the fabric when washed; an inch to a yard is usually enough, although when using unbleached cloths it is wise to allow three inches.

"Square up" fabric at either end by tearing or cutting along a thread.

Color matching in the middle of printing a length can be very difficult. Be careful to mix enough of each color to last to the end of the project.

Printed lengths should be dried thoroughly before finishing; five days is usually long enough for a heavy drapery fabric. When hanging fabric, take care not to stretch it out of shape.

Always press block-printed fabrics on the reverse side of the print. Particles of excess ink on the front of the print may be melted by the heat of the iron and carried along by it, blurring and smearing the design.

GENERAL PRINTING PROCEDURES

For most printing projects the general procedures are the same.

Cover the working surface of your table with a layer of newspapers that can be rolled up and thrown away when the printing session is over.

The palette should be clean and set close to the edge of the table, colors and solvents handy, along with spatulas and paint rags.

The printing table or bed should be dusted to get rid of bits of dirt, and spread with a fresh pad of newspapers. Lay out the paper or fabric to be printed smoothly on the padded bed. If necessary, pin the paper to the bed, or hold down the edges with a heavy ruler or T-square. Use a palette knife to lift a little of the color out of the container onto a corner of the palette. Both oil- and water-base printer's ink, and poster paint, are opaque. Therefore, to lighten any color white must be added. To make a color darker, add black or a darker color, such as a deep blue.

Dip the brayer into the ink lightly, then roll it back and forth on a clean section of the palette until the roller is evenly and completely covered with ink. Now roll the inky brayer lightly over the whole surface of the block that you are going to print.

Carefully lift the inked object and place it face down where you want to print it. Press down as hard as you can. If the printing bed is on the floor, step all over the back of the block. If working on a table, lean on the block or try hitting it with a rubber mallet, being careful to keep the block from slipping between blows. When you think enough pressure has been applied to make a clear print, lift the block straight up from the printing paper —behold your print!

Or if you are using a wooden block, there is another method of printing that allows you to control very exactly where the dark and light pattern of the print will be. The inked block remains face up on the table and the paper is placed on top of it. Using the back of a spoon, rub the paper gently until the print begins to come through. Rub firmly on those areas that you want to be strong and dark, and lightly on those that should be less strong. The paper is then gently peeled from the surface of the block.

No matter which method of printing you use, the block must be inked each time it is printed. Sometimes, however, you may want to experiment with a series of progressively lighter prints.

Glossary

The following glossary consists of terms commonly used in all forms of print making. Most of the terms appear in the text of this book; some, however, do not. The latter are presented in order to help the reader widen his horizons to include all forms of the rewarding techniques in print making.

aquatint—an etching technique used to create tone, somewhat as washes are used to create tone in pen-and-ink drawing. To aquatint, powdered rosin is dusted over the plate. The plate is then heated; the rosin fuses, leaving little pores through which acid can reach the plate.

brayer—a soft rubber roller mounted in a handle. A brayer is used to roll out printing ink and to transfer it in an even film to the block.

C-clamp—a C-shaped piece of metal with a screw mounted on one side. This tool was designed to hold wood in place, and is useful when cutting a wood block.

drypoint—an intaglio technique in which a sharp, round, needle-like point is used to scratch a design into a metal plate. As the point scratches into the plate, it raises a furrow. The furrow, called a burr, is usually rough and slightly irregular. This burr, not the scratched line, will receive and hold most of the ink. As a result, the typical drypoint line is soft, irregular, and velvety.

engraving—an intaglio technique in which slivers of metal are removed to form the lines which make up the image. As the engraving tool is worked across the surface of the plate, it scoops out a sliver of metal, leaving a V-shaped trench with little or no burr. The printed line is sharp and clean-cut.

etching—an intaglio technique in which lines are eroded in the surface of a metal plate. The plate is covered with an acid-resistant material and the artist scratches into this material, just lightly enough to expose the metal lying under it. The plate is then submerged in acid, and only the exposed parts of the plate are eaten away by the acid. The depth of line is controlled by the length of submersion.

gouge—a chisel with a curved, rather than flat, cutting edge. Various gouges produce U-shaped and V-shaped cuts of different depths.

intaglio printing process—a process in which the image or design to be printed is cut or etched into a metal plate, usually copper. To print such a plate, the plate is warmed and tacky ink is worked all over it. The plate is heated and then wiped; the depressed lines hold the ink, but the non-incised parts of the plate are wiped clean. The plate is then placed, face-up, on the bed of a printing press and damp paper is laid over it. Felt pads or blankets are placed over the paper, and the whole setup is run between two rollers. The resulting pressure forces the pads or blankets to crush the paper into the incised lines, and the ink transfers. The three major kinds of intaglio printing are drypoint, engraving, and etching.

key block—the block used as a guide for registering other blocks in color printing.

linocut—another term for linoleum print. The word is used more often in England than it is in the United States.

linoleum print or *linoleum cut*—a print taken from a relief carved in linoleum. A linoleum print may have a great deal of linear variety due to the ease of working in this smooth, easy-to-cut material.

mezzotint—a method of creating a print with a wide range of tones. In this process the surface of a metal plate is roughed up with a large, sharp tool called a rocker. The artist works from dark toward light by scraping and burnishing the roughed up areas. The tones in a mezzotint range from a dark, velvety black, through a wide variety of grays, to white.

monotype, or monoprint—a unique print
made by a means that permits only
one impression.
palette—any flat, nonabsorbent surface
which is large enough to hold ink or
paint and allow space for rolling out the
color.

plaster print or *plaster relief print*—
a print cast from an intaglio plate.
The print is actually a plaster cast made
by pouring liquid plaster of paris
over an inked plate. The finished product
is a black and white print in relief;
therefore, the term plaster relief is
preferred.
pounce—a soft ball of cotton or other
absorbent material used to dab ink on
small areas.
printing bed—any smooth, thick pad used
when printing relief blocks face down.

proof—a print taken from an
unfinished block.
relief printing process—a process in
which the image to be printed is created
in relief. A material like wood or
linoleum may be cut away to leave the
design in relief, or relief may be
built up on a flat surface by the addition
of cardboard cutouts or other materials.
silk screen—a type of stenciling. A
fine-mesh screen (frequently a piece of
silk) is stretched on a wooden frame.
All parts of the screen, except the
design, are made impermeable, and
liquid colors are then squeezed through
the permeable parts of the screen.
stencil—a thin sheet of sturdy material
perforated with a design or lettering.
The stencil is laid on a surface and
inked. The ink passes through the
perforations.

stop block—a gadget used to prevent a
woodblock from slipping while it is
being gouged.
woodcut—a print taken from a design
carved in a plank of wood; it often
retains the texture of the grain of the
plank.
wood engraving—a highly exacting
technique involving engraving on a
piece of polished endwood. Endwood,
which is a cross-cut section of wood,
has little or no perceptible grain. This
allows cutting delicate lines in any
direction. Wood engraving was widely
used for graphic reproduction before
the advent of photomechanical processe

Acknowledgments

The authors are grateful to the many
print makers who generously gave
permission to reproduce their work, and to
those art teachers who took time from
their crowded schedules to send us
examples of work done under supervision.
We want particularly to thank Calvin
Burnett for allowing us to use the work of
some of his graphics students at the
Massachusetts College of Art, Boston;
Philip Dolan, art supervisor in the
town of Weymouth, Massachusetts;
Anthony Lopes, artist and junior
high school art teacher in Worcester,
Massachusetts; and Jeanette Rich, art
supervisor in Charlemont, Massachusetts.

   Albert Jacobson, artist and potter,
whose clay prints are unique; Jane Craig,
"The Potato Printer"; Margaret
Philbrick, who shared the results of her
experience cutting Masonite blocks;
and Sylvia Mazur Rantz, faithful
secretary of the Boston Printmakers, were
also very helpful. Fred Niebergal took
the "how-to" photographs of children at
The Shady Hill School, Cambridge,
Massachusetts.

   No one can teach without students,
and we are grateful for the co-operation of
all our students, past and present, at
The Shady Hill School; The Cummington
School of the Arts in Cummington,
Massachusetts; the Willimantic Summer
Arts and Crafts Workshop, Willimantic,
Connecticut; the Boston YWCA Craft
Workshop; and the State University
College for Teachers at Buffalo,
New York.

   But above all, we must acknowledge
that we could never have come close
to completing this manuscript without the
ungrudgingly given help and critical
acumen of our husbands, Hal Sproul and
Eric Erickson, and the uncritical
patience of the assorted children in our
two households.